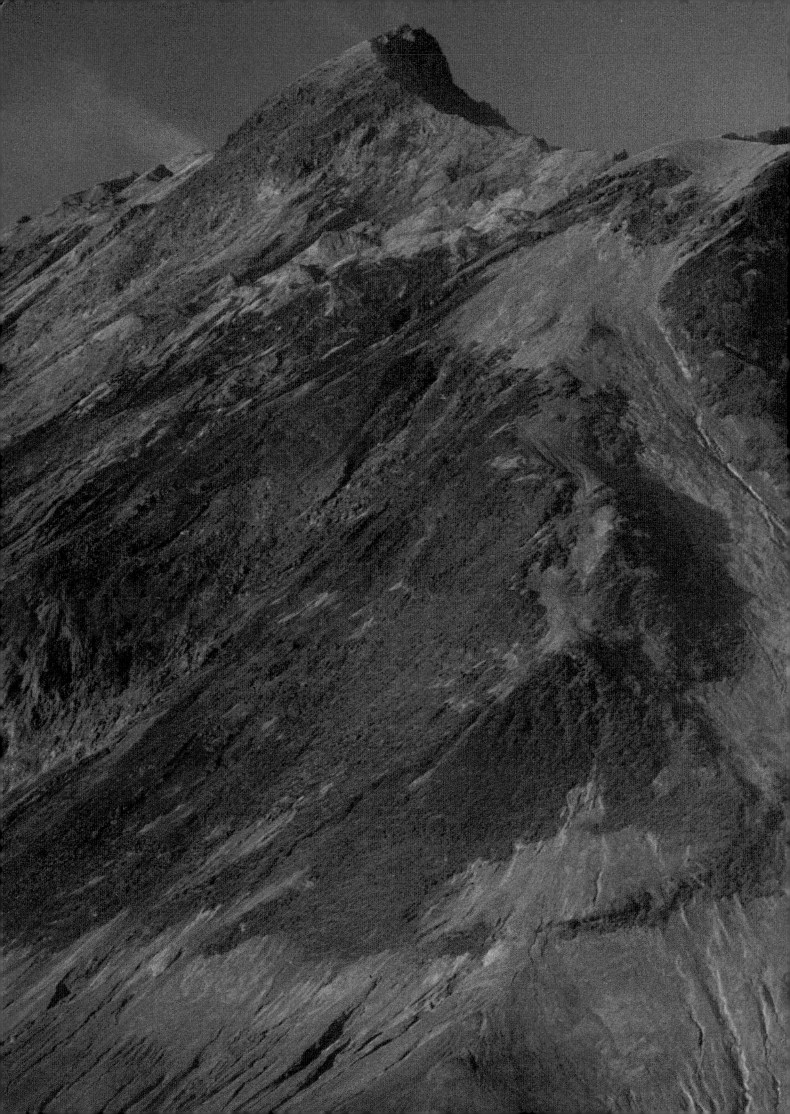

MOUNT ST. HELENS

The Eruption and Recovery of a Volcano

Rob Carson

With selected photographs by

Geff Hinds

Cheryl Haselhorst

and Gary Braasch

SASQUATCH BOOKS
SEATTLE

With *The News Tribune*, Tacoma, Washington

©1990, ©2000 by *The News Tribune*
All rights reserved. No parts of this book may be
reprinted without the written permission of the
publisher.

Library of Congress Cataloging in Publication Data
Carson, Rob 1950–
Mount St. Helens: The eruption and recovery of a
volcano / Rob Carson.
   p. cm.
ISBN 1-57061-248-X
Natural history—Washington (State)—Saint Helens,
Mount. 2. Ecology—Washington (State)—Saint
Helens, Mount. 3. Saint Helens, Mount (Wash.)—
Eruption, 1980—Environmental aspects.
1. Title.
QH105.W2C37 1990
508.797'84—dc20

Cover photo: ©1980 Gary Braasch/CORBIS
Cover design: Kate Basart
Interior design and production: Marquand Books, Inc.
Typesetting: The Type Gallery, Inc.
Printed and bound in Hong Kong by Toppan
Printing Co., Ltd.

Published by Sasquatch Books
615 Second Avenue, Suite 260
Seattle, WA 98104
(206) 467-4300
books@SasquatchBooks.com
www.SasquatchBooks.com

PHOTO CREDITS

1	The News Tribune
2–3	Geff Hinds
5	Peter Frenzen, USFS
6–7	Geff Hinds
8–9	Bob and Ira Spring
10	Ray Atkeson
11	All: U.S. Geological Survey
12	Top left: Bob Rudsit
12–13	Center: Geff Hinds
13	Top: Bruce Kellman
14	Geff Hinds
14	Inset: Ray Atkeson
15	Bob and Ira Spring
16–17	Geff Hinds
18	Ray Atkeson
19	Top: Stark Museum of Art, Orange, Texas
20–21	All: University of Washington Libraries
22–23	Ray Atkeson
24–28	All: Gary Rosenquist
30–31	All: Cheryl Haselhorst
32	Cheryl Haselhorst
33	Geff Hinds
34	Cheryl Haselhorst
35	Bruce Kellman
36	Bob Rudsit
37	Bob Rudsit
38	Top inset: Weyerhaeuser Company
38	Bottom inset: Weyerhaeuser Company
38–39	Bob Rudsit
40–41	*Seattle Weekly*
43	Full page: Cheryl Haselhorst
43	Middle inset: *Seattle Weekly*
43	Bottom inset: Cheryl Haselhorst
44–45	Geff Hinds
46	Geff Hinds
47	Top inset: Geff Hinds
47	Bottom: Cheryl Haselhorst
48	Top inset: Cheryl Haselhorst
48	Middle inset: Russ Carmack
48	Bottom inset: Cheryl Haselhorst
48–49	Cheryl Haselhorst
50–51	All: Cheryl Haselhorst
52	Top: Colleen Gray
52–53	Center: Cheryl Haselhorst
53	Top: Cheryl Haselhorst
54–55	Philip Amdal / Westock
55	Top inset: Douglas Miller / Westock
55	Middle inset: Phil Schofield / Westock
55	Bottom inset: Gary Braasch, © 1990
57	Cheryl Haselhorst
58	Gary Braasch, © 1990
58	Inset: Geff Hinds
60	John Scott
61	*Seattle Weekly*
62–63	Geff Hinds
63	Inset: Cheryl Haselhorst
64–65	Center: Cheryl Haselhorst
65	Top: Colleen Gray
67	All: Cheryl Haselhorst
68	Center: Cheryl Haselhorst
68–69	Illustrations: Colleen Gray
70–71	All: Cheryl Haselhorst
72	Geff Hinds
73	Top: Cheryl Haselhorst
73	Inset: Geff Hinds
75	Full page: Geff Hinds
75	Inset: Gary Braasch, © 1990
76–77	Geff Hinds
78–79	All: Gary Braasch, © 1990
80–81	Gary Braasch, © 1990
82	Gary Braasch, © 1990
84–85	Cheryl Haselhorst
86–87	All: Geff Hinds
88–89	Geff Hinds
90	Geff Hinds
90	Inset: Weyerhaeuser Company
91	Geff Hinds
92–93	Geff Hinds
94	Geff Hinds
95	Geff Hinds
96–97	All: Geff Hinds
98–99	Geff Hinds
98	Top inset: Geff Hinds
98	Bottom inset: Bob Rudsit
100–101	All: Geff Hinds
102–103	All: Geff Hinds
104–105	Geff Hinds
106	Geff Hinds
106	Top inset: Cheryl Haselhorst
106	Middle inset: Geff Hinds
106	Bottom inset: Geff Hinds
107	Geff Hinds
108–109	Weyerhaeuser Company
110	Geff Hinds
111	Top: Cheryl Haselhorst
111	Inset: Geff Hinds
111	Bottom: Geff Hinds
112–113	All: Cheryl Haselhorst
114–115	Top: Cheryl Haselhorst
114	Bottom left: Weyerhaueser Company
114	Bottom right: Weyerhaeuser Company
116–117	Geff Hinds
118	Cheryl Haselhorst
118–119	Bottom inset: Weyerhaeuser Company
119	Cheryl Haselhorst
120–121	All: Cheryl Haselhorst
122	All: Cheryl Haselhorst
124–125	All: Geff Hinds
126–127	All: Cheryl Haselhorst
129	Top: Weyerhaeuser Company
128–129	Center: Cheryl Haselhorst
130	Geff Hinds
130–131	Geff Hinds
131	Top inset: Weyerhaeuser Company
131	Bottom inset: Bob and Ira Spring
132–133	Geff Hinds
134–135	All: Geff Hinds
136	Top: Jim Quiring, USFS
136	Bottom: Gary Braasch, © 1999
137	All: Jim Quiring, USFS
138-139	Gary Braasch, © 1990
140	Two left: Peter Frenzen, USFS
140–141	Center: Gary Braasch, © 1999
141	Right: Peter Frenzen, USFS
142	All: Gary Braasch, © 1990
143	Gary Braasch, © 1989
144	Gary Braasch, © 1999
146	Gary Braasch, © 1984
147	Gary Braasch, © 1999
149	All: Peter Frenzen, USFS
150	Gary Braasch, © 1999
151	Gary Braasch, © 1999
153	Peter Frenzen, USFS
154–155	Gary Braasch, © 1999
157	Gary Braasch, © 1990

All photographs by Cheryl Haselhorst were
originally taken for *The Columbian*,
Vancouver, Washington

CONTENTS

ACKNOWLEDGMENTS

This book was conceived as a way to commemorate the tenth anniversary of the cataclysmic eruption of Mount St. Helens on May 18, 1980, and as an opportunity to acknowledge the discoveries made by scientists who have worked in the blast zone since that time. The credit for that original inspiration belongs to Jan Brandt, assistant managing editor of *The Morning News Tribune* in Tacoma, Washington. Credit also belongs to the *The Morning News Tribune*'s publisher, Bill Honeysett, for having enough faith in the project to put the resources of his company behind it.

The book would have been impossible without the help of the scientists who have done research at Mount St. Helens. Without exception they were generous and patient in sharing their knowledge. In particular, thanks goes to "Mr. Crater," Don Swanson, at the U.S. Geological Survey, for serving as an intrepid guide not only to the crater of Mount St. Helens, but also through the labyrinth of scientific knowledge that has been compiled about it. Special thanks also goes to Charles Crisafulli, ecologist at the Mount St. Helens National Volcanic Monument, for sharing his excitement about the return of life to the blast zone and for his willingness, far beyond expectation, to loan his extensive collection of Mount St. Helens research papers and journal articles. Peter Frenzen, monument scientist; USGS geologist Steven Brantley; University of Washington geophysicist Steven Malone; Jerry Franklin, chief plant ecologist for the U.S. Forest Service's Pacific Northwest Research Station; and U.W. seismic analyst Christine Jonientz-Trisler aided the project immeasurably with their insights, memories, and encouragement.

Suki Dardarian, the editor and manager of this project, handled the logistics with the aplomb of an air-traffic controller, offered sound editorial advice that helped shape the book, and gave invaluable moral support from beginning to end. The wise Sam Angeloff helped with advice and encouragement during the initial phases. Susan Cunningham, reference specialist at the Pacific Northwest Collection of the Special Collections Division of the University of Washington's Suzzallo Library, saved a great deal of time with her guidance to the library's mountain of St. Helens material.

Joan Gregory contributed a keen editorial eye and an unrelenting sense of logic during the final editing of the manuscript. Anne Depue and Chad Haight of Sasquatch Books were unfailingly supportive and professional.

Thanks to Lyn Smallwood and Theodora Ruth Carson, who in the course of this project discovered the mixed blessings of having a husband and father who works at home. And finally, a nod to mountain man and surveyor Tom LaGra, of Randle, Washington, who first introduced me to the old-growth forests that once surrounded Mount St. Helens. We never dreamed they would all be lost.

Rob Carson
February 1990

When the first edition of this book appeared 10 years ago, Mount St. Helens was still warm and smoking. Scientists still were not sure the violent eruptive cycle that began in 1980 had ended, and they were just beginning to realize what an extraordinary opportunity the mountain offered as a natural laboratory.

Twenty years is but an instant in the life of a volcano—but it has been time enough to reflect and observe, to make discoveries about how the natural world works and the place of human beings within it. This new edition attempts to document those discoveries, to remark once again not only on the overwhelming power of the natural world but also on its reassuring continuity. It is intended as a tribute to the canniness and determination of the life forces that simultaneously transform the world and keep it the same.

Rob Carson
December 1999

PARADISE LOST

On May 17, 1980, Mount St. Helens was a symmetrical cone, a mountain so near perfection it was sometimes called "America's Mount Fujiyama." Photographers loved St. Helens because it looked the way a mountain is supposed to look: smooth sides, pointed crest, fluted topping of snow. At its base, a clear, blue-green lake reflected an upside-down image of the mountain precisely enough to cause vertigo. It was a scene made for calendars and postcards.

That was May 17. By the evening of May 18, Mount St. Helens was a smoking crater, hollowed-out and grey. It looked defiled, like the victim of some grisly crime. Mount St. Helens had burst into volcanic eruption at 8:32 that morning, exploding sideways with a blast so powerful it knocked down trees 17 miles away. When the ash cleared, the mountain had dropped in rank from Washington's fifth-highest peak, at 9,677 feet, to its thirtieth-highest, at 8,364 feet. Fanning out to the north was a 234-square-mile swath of destruction so bleak it defied earthly comparisons. The analogies that fit best were extraterrestrial ones. As then-President Jimmy Carter noted, along with many of the journalists who rushed to the scene from as far away as New Zealand and Japan, the zone of destruction resembled the surface of the moon.

Pulverized bits of the mountain, driven by hurricane-force winds, had stripped the soil from nearby ridges and hillsides, leaving bare rock. Every plant was either vaporized or torn from the surface. Clear mountain lakes were transformed into tea-colored swamps, littered with broken trees. Miles from the volcano, entire forests lay scattered like straw, the fallen tree trunks sandblasted smooth. Volcanic ash, finer than beach sand, shrouded parts of four states. Fifty-seven people were dead, along with millions of birds, deer, elk, and fish.

What was most unusual about the eruption of Mount St. Helens, aside from the lateral direction of the blast, was that it had taken place in a developed country, clearly visible from the skyscrapers and universities of the Northwest's two largest cities. The eruption was regarded as a disaster, but as an opportunity, too. It was a window into the earth, transportation through time to an exotic, primordial era. People rushed to the mountain, fascinated and horrified at the same time. In the days after the blast, news photographers fought for access to helicopters; scientists, would-be scientists, tourists, and reporters stormed the barricades set up around the edges of the blast zone, wheedling, cajoling, threatening guards to let them in. Mount St. Helens was the most closely watched, most-photographed, and best scientifically documented volcanic eruption in history.

The image of Mount St. Helens shimmers in the clear, cold water of Spirit Lake.

Above: Mount St. Helens hurls steam and ash thousands of feet into the sky over downtown Portland, where it joins clouds from two earlier eruptions. *Right, top and bottom:* High-altitude, infrared views of Mount St. Helens taken from a NASA U-2 aircraft, before and after the May 18, 1980, eruption. The first picture was taken on May 2, the second on June 19. Red color indicates living vegetation. Checkered patterns in the "before" picture are from clear-cut logging.

Afterward, a seemingly insatiable market developed for volcano memorabilia: volcanic ash pottery, bumper stickers, T-shirts, postcards, and picture books. Portland Community College offered a class titled "How to Paint Pictures with Volcanic Ash." So many people mailed samples of ash to friends across the country that the spillage from broken packages jammed letter-sorting equipment in post offices. Cars caught in the blast, their taillights and dashboard instruments melted into hanging globules of plastic, became tourist attractions. So did ruined homes. In the mud-choked Toutle River valley, one enterprising man whose home had been spared, hung a sign on the house of his not-so-lucky neighbor: "Walk Through the Buried A-Frame!" A man from Cleveland, Ohio, called the Cowlitz County Sheriff's Department to offer a young woman as a human sacrifice to appease the volcano gods.

The amount of land destroyed in the eruption was not that vast when viewed in context. It amounted to less than 0.7 percent of the forested land in Washington state. If the entire state were a checkerboard, the blast zone would have fit easily into one-quarter of one red square. But the psychological impacts were much larger. The eruption changed the way people structured their personal histories; it was a fulcrum in the span of time, an event of such magnitude that others were measured by it. People who were living in the Pacific Northwest in 1980 remember where they were and what they were doing when the mountain blew as clearly as they remember the bombing of Pearl Harbor or the assassination of John F. Kennedy.

Mount St. Helens altered the way Northwesterners regarded their surroundings, bringing an element of insecurity to a region where nature had seemed unusually benevolent. The volcano caused people to call into question some strongly held beliefs: that mountains are eternal, for example, and that nature is benign. The Cascade peaks, lined up like innocent dollops of whipped cream from California to British Columbia, were suddenly seen as threats. People were made painfully aware that nature can be unpredictable—and deadly.

"If the Holocaust didn't do it, the blast of this mountain would have flattened any remnant of faith based on the natural world," the Reverend Arthur Morgan, a minister from the nearby town of Kelso, wrote shortly after the eruption. "Such a faith has been rendered absurd. In a world where mountains wash into the sea, our marriage, job, economy, and government appear all the more vulnerable. What remains secure?"

Morgan's own faith may have been shaken, but it was not destroyed. The true foundation, he said, was rebirth: Flowers were bursting out of the ash a week after the eruption. "It is this push of life toward life that allows us to speak of God," he said. "Despite the apparent eternal beauty of the lakes, and everlasting appearance of the mountains, the only certainty is the spirit of life which is greater than all of these things."

Others did not find the connection so easy to make. Studies on the psychological effects of the eruption on communities close to Mount St. Helens indicated widespread depression that in some cases persisted for years after the blast. People suffered from troubled sleep, jumpiness, irritability, and a sense of powerlessness. They felt rage, hopelessness, and grief over the death of friends and family, and guilt that they themselves had survived.

Psychologists differ on the subject, but most believe that such post-traumatic stresses don't last long. People tend to wrap themselves in more comfortable thoughts; the impact of disaster is gradually diluted until it disappears.

Nature, likewise, heals its wounds. According to biologists, in 100 years it will be difficult to see any effects of the volcanic devastation. The most lasting impacts of the Mount St. Helens eruption may be those that have occurred in the realm of science. After the explosion, the volcano and the devastated area surrounding it became a vast, outdoor laboratory for biologists and geologists from around the world. Observing the interactions of species that struggled back into the blast zone has led to revelations about the very nature of life.

Left and center: The volcano inspired seemingly limitless bursts of entrepreneurship. Sensing the opportunity for profit, residents of the surrounding area lined highways with makeshift hot-dog stands and souvenir shops. *Above:* The hood of a car is transformed into an airbrushed artifact.

The volcano caused stunning metamorphoses in the landscape, creating stark, alien worlds near the summit (*left*), and a new, low profile across the waters of Yale Lake (*inset*). *Above:* The post-eruption view of the mountain from a ridge in the Gifford Pinchot National Forest is a sobering transformation from the former vista of snowy peak framed by centuries-old trees.

The eruption also led to revelations in volcanology. By watching Mount St. Helens and monitoring every shudder and exhalation before and after the blast, geologists gained a better understanding of how volcanoes work. As a direct result of the eruption, the U.S. Geological Survey established a major volcano-research center in Vancouver, Washington—the David A. Johnston Cascades Volcano Observatory—which now serves as a base for monitoring all of the Cascade Range volcanoes and an international center for volcano research.

The brand of science practiced at the observatory is still in its infancy. In 1792, when George Vancouver and his crew first sighted Mount St. Helens from the deck of the *Discovery*, many Europeans still clung to the notion that volcanoes were caused by burning coal, deep underground. Others, in that more religious age, believed that volcanoes were gateways to the infernal regions and imagined Lucifer sitting enthroned in the flames. The lava that burst forth from volcanoes was believed to come from the fires of hell, and the noise from the shrieks and groans of damned souls.

That view was not significantly different from those held by native Northwest Indians. The native people, whose ancestors had occupied the land around the Cascade Range for perhaps 10,000 years before the Europeans arrived, regarded Mount St. Helens with a mixture of fear and awe, as might be expected for a mountain that periodically sent great plumes into the heavens and caused large quantities of ash to fall from the sky. The native people who lived in the shadow of the mountain—the Salish-speaking tribes to the north and west, the Cowlitz to the southwest, and the Klickitats to the south and east—believed that volcanic outbursts were divine retribution for their own personal failings or fallout from warring spirit gods. They called the mountain Loo-wit ("Keeper of the Fire"), Lawelatla ("One from Whom Smoke Comes"), or Tah-one-lat-clah ("Fire Mountain").

Northwest Indians generally stayed away from Mount St. Helens, believing that approaching it would pose a risk not only to themselves, but to all life. There is no indication that any native person climbed to the summit of Mount St. Helens—or any other Northwest volcano—before Europeans arrived. Apparently, the only time tribal members would even go near the mountain was on the occasions of spirit quests. Young men would venture to the tree line, and there, knees shaking and hearts pounding, they would absorb mana from the Great Spirit within.

According to John Staps, a Klickitat Indian who led a party of whites to the summit of Mount St. Helens in 1860 (and lived the rest of his life in

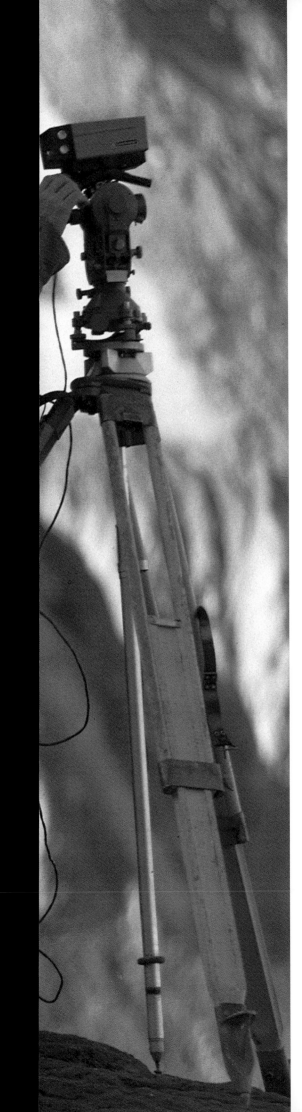

shame for having done so), "When an Indian boy wished to be received into the council of the brave of his nation, he would ascend the mountain peak as far up as the grass grows and there prove his bravery by walking to and fro, in [the] presence of the Spirit which governs the mountain, until morning. His return to his people was hailed with every demonstration of delight. Old men and brave warriors greeted him and welcomed him into their secret councils. He was no longer a *tenas man* [adolescent], but a great brave."

Spirit Lake, the blue-green mirror at the base of the volcano, also was rarely visited. Canadian artist Paul Kane, who traveled through the Northwest during the 1840s, reported that Cowlitz Indians believed Mount St. Helens was "inhabited by a race of beings of a different species who are cannibals and whom they hold in great dread; they also say that there is a lake at its base with a very extraordinary kind of fish in it, with a head more resembling that of a bear than any other animal." The lake was regarded as a sort of purgatory, to which the souls of the most wicked, blasphemous, and cruel people who ever lived were banished.

The Cowlitz, Coast Salish, and Klickitats all had legends that starred Mount St. Helens, with lesser roles for its close neighbors in the Cascade Range—Mount Hood, Mount Adams, and Mount Rainier. The specifics of the native mythologies and lore vary, but the tales have certain basic elements in common. In the legend most often repeated, two brothers (Mount Hood and Mount Adams) fall in love with a shapely maiden (Mount St. Helens) and fight over her. The rivalry between the brothers becomes violent: Smoke and fire fill the sky. Thunderbolts crash down from above. The sun is blotted out. Rivers turn brown. Animals flee in terror. St. Helens tries to stop the fighting but fails. Finally, all three mountains fall exhausted to the earth. The Great Spirit arrives, highly irritated. He rewards St. Helens for her bravery by turning her into a beautiful, shapely mountain again, a young mountain with an ancient and knowledgeable soul.

The basic geology underlying these tales is fairly consistent with what actually happened. Geologists believe Hood and Adams may in fact have erupted at approximately the same time, causing widespread damage to the landscape. Eruptions on Mount St. Helens transformed the mountain from a symmetrical cone to rubble and back to symmetry again at least three times, the last transformation occurring in the past 2,000 years. It wasn't until the 1960s that the non-native occupants of the Northwest came to those conclusions through geological mapping of old mudflows and ash deposits.

After the eruption, scientists from around the world converged on Mount St. Helens and the surrounding blast zone, eager to take advantage of research opportunities. Here, USGS geologist Gene Iwatsubo monitors the changing shape of the volcano in order to predict future activity.

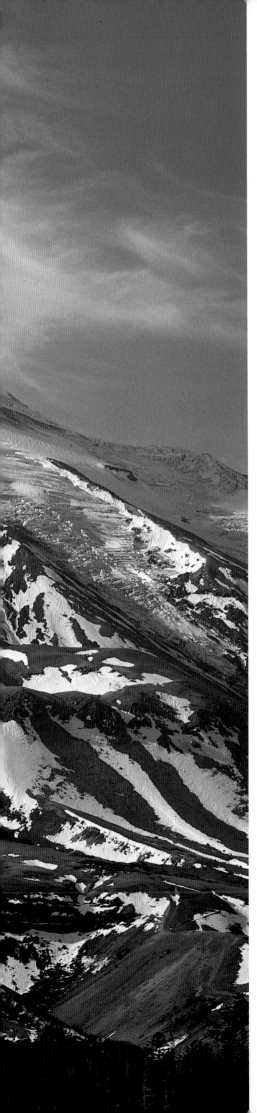

By the time the Northwest was settled in the mid-nineteenth century, scientists had established that volcanoes were caused by molten rock welling up from the hot interior of the earth. Volcanoes had come to be regarded dispassionately enough that when farmers and missionaries saw clouds of steam over Mount St. Helens in the 1830s, they considered the event more a curiosity than a sign, either of heavenly wrath or earthly danger. Illogically, Mount St. Helens was not thought to be the same kind of volcano as Vesuvius and Krakatoa. The fact that the Cascade peaks were volcanoes was regarded as interesting, but only slightly more relevant than the last ice age.

In 1853, near the end of St. Helens's last active period before 1980, Thomas J. Dryer, editor of Portland's *The Oregonian*, led the first successful ascent of Mount St. Helens. For a trained journalist, Dryer offered precious little insight into the experience. Upon viewing the mountain from above tree line on its south slope, he said it was "sublimely grand and impossible to describe." The view from the top, which he and the four members of his party experienced while gasping from lack of oxygen—their ears ringing and noses bleeding from the altitude—he captured only slightly more vividly: "It would be futile to attempt to give our readers a correct idea of the appearance of the vast extent of the country visible from the top of the mountain," Dryer wrote. "The ocean, distant over one hundred miles, was plainly seen. The whole Coast and Cascade ranges of mountains could be plainly traced with the naked eye. The snow-covered peaks of Mts. Hood, Rainier, and two others seemed close by. These form a sort of amphitheater on a large scale, diversified with hills and valleys."

At that time, St. Helens rose from a centuries-old evergreen forest so dense that sunlight filtered dimly through the canopy. The forest floor was spongy with rotted trees and mosses; clear streams ran through the woods and open meadows and collected in cold, transparent lakes. Spirit Lake, the largest of these, was heavily populated with salmon and steelhead that migrated up the Columbia River from the Pacific Ocean.

The glacier-capped cone of Mount St. Helens was a foreboding sight to native Americans, who regarded the mountain as a powerful spiritual force. *Above:* The painting *Mount St. Helens Erupting* (1847) by Paul Kane, in the collection of the Stark Museum of Art, Orange, Texas. *Left:* Features visible in this late-summer shot of the north face are Dog's Head (the prominent bulge on the upper left), Forsyth Glacier, Sugar Bowl (lower right), Little Lizard, and Big Lizard (the two ridges creeping up the right flank).

At the turn of the century, Mount St. Helens was a popular destination for Northwest climbers. *Above:* Members of the Oregon Alpine Club relax on the peak on July 26, 1889, posing for what is believed to be the first photograph ever taken on the summit. *Below:* The Mountaineers from Seattle, climbing en masse in 1917, descend the snowy slopes using alpenstocks for balance, and (*bottom*) take a break at the base of the Forsyth Glacier. *Right:* The Mountaineers explore Harmony Falls on the east arm of Spirit Lake.

As was the pattern throughout the history of the American West, the initial exploration of the Mount St. Helens area was followed quickly by exploitation. Commercial timber cutting began in the Toutle River valley in the 1880s, and by 1895 a logging railroad on the valley floor was hauling timber downriver from eight logging camps. The trail up the north fork of the river to Spirit Lake was widened and smoothed into a wagon road in 1901 to serve copper miners who had staked claims just north of Spirit Lake on Paradise Creek.

As the population of the territory grew and roads improved, Mount St. Helens became a popular destination for mountaineers. Climbing the peak required some stamina, but not much in the way of technical knowledge. Shortly after the turn of the century, members of the Mazamas, a Portland mountaineering club, regularly ascended the peak in groups of 50 or more. They packed equipment up the rutted wagon road from Castle Rock to Spirit Lake, and carrying alpenstocks and wearing sun hats and snow goggles, they trudged single file to the top.

In 1909, the Portland YMCA built a summer camp on the south shore of the lake where children could fish, hike, and paddle canoes. For campers, the trip to the mountain was an adventure in itself: In those days it meant a steamboat ride down the Columbia River to Kelso, a train to Castle Rock, and then a long, bumpy wagon ride up the Toutle River to the south shore of Spirit Lake. Later, the Boy Scouts, Girl Scouts, and the Episcopal church also built camps on the lake. Thousands remember Mount St. Helens from their days as campers—hikes in the dark mossy forest, campfire sing-alongs, hearing and half-believing stories about apelike Sasquatches who snatched campers from their bunks and hauled them off to their lairs to eat. They remember boat rides from the south shore when the snowy crest of Mount St. Helens would peek over the tops of trees and then expand to fill the sky as the boat moved across the lake; they remember breath-stopping plunges into the icy lake, kerosene lanterns glowing orange in cabin windows, the way the first rays of sun caught the top of St. Helens and gave it a rosy glow.

The mountain quickly lost its solitude. As early as 1938, 26,000 people visited Mount St. Helens in the summer season, including 2,250 on a single weekend. The road to Spirit Lake was paved in 1946, and each year after that the steady march of house trailers and A-frames crept farther and farther up the Toutle River and its tributaries. A paved road was built to the timberline in 1962 with the intention of developing a ski area on the mountain (the idea was abandoned because of the avalanche danger). On clear weekends in the 1970s, it was routine for as many as 500 people to climb to the summit of the volcano. Spirit Lake was the most heavily used recreation site in the Gifford Pinchot National Forest, which encompasses Mount St. Helens. One hundred private cabins ringed the lake.

Meanwhile, the pace of logging increased. By 1970 virtually all forests on state and private land near Mount St. Helens had been cut and hauled away. The Forest Service, manager of most of the old-growth timber still standing, launched an ambitious program of road building and logging that reached high on the mountain's flanks, even in places where regeneration was a rec- ognized impossibility. In 1949 there were 655 miles of logging roads in the Gifford Pinchot National Forest; by 1980 there were 3,700 miles of roads.

In the late 1970s, environmental groups launched a major effort to save the remnants of old-growth forest around the mountain, lobbying Congress to provide protective legislation. The move was bitterly contested by the timber industry and the Forest Service, and by 1980 the controversy had escalated into a major land-use battle.

And then, on the afternoon of March 20, 1980, seismologists at the Uni- versity of Washington recorded a magnitude 4.0 earthquake directly under the mountain, the first jolt of an ominous trembling that gradually increased in strength and frequency over the next few days. A small crater opened near the mountain's summit on March 27, and during the next seven weeks, pre- liminary bursts of steam and ash hissed into the sky.

Mount St. Helens was about to apply its own solution to the land-use problem.

Right: Members of the Portland YMCA, staying at Camp Meehan on the northern tip of Spirit Lake, raise their voices in a 1940s campfire sing-along as the sun washes the summit of Mount St. Helens in the day's last light. Several youth camps dotted the 12-mile shoreline of the lake, the setting for fond childhood memories of thousands of Northwesterners.

May 1980. The idea was to get dynamite pictures of the awakening volcano and sell them to tourists. To do that, Gary Rosenquist would have to get clear of all the crowds that had been gathering for several weeks on the south and west sides of Mount St. Helens. He would also have to find a way around the National Guardsmen who were stopping traffic on the two main routes to the mountain—the Spirit Lake Highway out of Castle Rock and State Route 503 up the south side through Cougar. The best bet seemed to be the gravel logging roads that wound from clearcut to clearcut out of the little town of Randle on the north side of the mountain. One of Gary's buddies, Joel Harvey, said he knew where there was a perfect view of the peak—a place where the mountain looked so close you could almost reach out and touch it.

Rosenquist, an unemployed taxi driver from Tacoma, had a tripod and camera he'd been using to shoot pictures of Mount St. Helens ever since the first steam and ash began exploding from the mountain in late March. So far, he'd been unable to get the close-up shots he wanted.

On Saturday, May 17, Rosenquist, Joel Harvey, Harvey's wife, Linda, their 10-year-old son Jo-Jo, and their neighbor, William Dilley, crammed themselves and their camping gear into Harvey's station wagon and set off for Randle. It was a clear, warm spring day, perfect for taking pictures. Sunday was supposed to be the same.

In Randle, they cut off on National Forest roads and drove to a ridgetop 10 miles from the mountain, a place called Bear Meadow. From there they had a straight shot at the peak. It towered over them, looking dark and sinister, its normally pure-white sides black with ash.

Rosenquist set up the camera and snapped a few shots. The mountain showed no signs of distress. They pitched the tent, and when it got dark, sat around a campfire talking. The night was clear, the sky filled with stars.

The next morning—May 18—the rising sun turned the mountain golden brown. Rosenquist set up the camera and tripod. Everything was quiet. "It felt like something was going to happen," Jo-Jo remembered later. "There was no noise, no animals—it was like a dream."

At 8:26 a.m., Rosenquist was back at the fire, eating breakfast. Dilley yelled at him from the ridge. "Something's happening!"

Rosenquist ran to his camera. The mountain looked exactly the same as it had earlier—except it seemed a little bit fuzzy, as if dust were blowing around on top.

8:27:00 a.m.

8:32:33 a.m.

8:32:37 a.m.

26

8:32:44 a.m.

8:32:48 a.m.

8:32:59 a.m.

Nervous, he bumped the tripod with his leg as he fired the first shot. He looked at the mountain more closely. Something was definitely happening. He took another picture, then stared in disbelief. Half the mountain had turned to a brown, churning liquid. A jet-black plume shot out the top.

"There it goes!" Dilley yelled. Rosenquist squeezed the shutter again. The black plume spilled into the sky. Below it, a dirty, brown cloud boiled up, forming surreal cauliflowers in the air.

The five of them stood transfixed as the cloud grew. Instead of settling back down, it kept getting bigger. "Let's get out of here!" Harvey yelled.

Rosenquist snapped another picture. The clouds were boiling, galloping straight for them. He grabbed his camera and they all ran for the station wagon. Dilley scrambled in through the back door and crouched on top of the camping gear.

As they spun onto the road, Rosenquist fired his last shot. The cloud was almost upon them. It thundered over the ridge separating them from the mountain, and loomed over them, blocking out the sun.

Rosenquist started rummaging in the glove box for more film. "No, no, man," Harvey yelled. "Help me drive." The car was sliding on the gravel and the road kept disappearing, even with the headlights on. Rocks the size of marbles spattered down on the roof. The trees whipped back and forth. Lightning flashed. Hot mud and ash poured out of the sky. The light disappeared. Harvey stopped the car. "This is it," he told himself.

Jo-Jo was crying. "Daddy, are we going to die?" In the back, Dilley was talking to God, promising to be good for the rest of his life if only he could survive.

Then the storm passed. The sky was filled with ash, but there was enough light for them to see the road. They continued on, finally reaching Randle and safety. Harvey reached over, patted the camera, and smiled at Rosenquist. "I think we got it," he said.

The series of pictures Rosenquist took that day became the most famous images of the eruption of Mount St. Helens. They showed the step-by-step disintegration of the mountain, the aerial launch of more than one-half a cubic mile of rock, and the origin of the hurricane of stones and ash that turned 234 square miles of verdant forest into a grey, windswept desert.

THE ERUPTION OF MOUNT ST. HELENS

On Thursday afternoon, March 20, two months before the devastating blast, a graduate student working in the geophysics laboratory at the University of Washington in Seattle was monitoring seismic readings routinely transmitted from Mount St. Helens. He noticed that an earthquake measuring a magnitude 4.0 on the Richter scale had originated at a point that appeared to be directly under the mountain. That was interesting—it was the strongest recorded earthquake in the southern Cascade Range since monitoring equipment had been installed there seven years earlier. But it was not remarkable.

The National Earthquake Information Center in Denver issued a routine press release, but most newspapers in the Pacific Northwest ignored it. President Jimmy Carter had announced the U.S. boycott of the Moscow Olympics the same day, and that story monopolized the news.

Aftershocks persisted the following day, as was expected, but on Saturday the number of earthquakes began to increase rather than tapering off. This was highly unusual.

The earthquakes occurred with increasing frequency on Sunday, and although monitoring techniques that indicate depth were not entirely reliable, the epicenters appeared to be rising gradually toward the surface. Excitement in the lab started to build. Thanks to a remarkably prescient report published in 1978 by U.S. Geological Survey geologists Dwight "Rocky" Crandell and Donal Mullineaux, everyone in the geophysics department knew that an eruption of Mount St. Helens was a very real possibility.

By Monday, March 24, the number of small earthquakes had jumped to more than one per minute, some as strong as 4.4 on the Richter scale. The seismograph needles twitched constantly. There was no doubt by then that something highly unusual was occurring beneath the mountain.

"The first thing I did when I came in Monday morning was call the USGS in Denver, where the volcanic hazards people were," said U.W. seismologist Steve Malone. "I talked to Rocky Crandell and told him I thought there was something significant going on at St. Helens.

"Rocky said, 'Don't worry about it. Those earthquakes are 30 kilometers away from the mountain.' He was using data from different stations than we were and couldn't tell where the earthquakes were coming from with as much accuracy. I said, 'Wrong. These suckers are right under the mountain.' "

Geologist Mullineaux was on a plane to Washington state the next day, and throughout the week more USGS geologists arrived with additional monitoring equipment and expertise. David Johnston, a young USGS geochemist and self-proclaimed volcano junkie, began working in the U.W. geophysics lab, helping interpret seismic readings. Don Swanson, an expert in predicting volcanic eruptions by measuring how mountains change shape before a blast, flew north from USGS Western Region Headquarters in Menlo Park, California.

The seismologists at the University of Washington issued a cautious press release, couched in the most guarded terms, warning that an eruption was a slight possibility. Five years earlier, warnings about a new steam vent on Mount Baker had led to extensive press coverage but no eruption, a scenario nobody wanted to repeat.

Representatives from the USGS, the Washington State Patrol, and the Washington State Department of Emergency Services held a five-hour meeting in Vancouver on Tuesday, March 25, to discuss the situation. The Forest Service sealed off the mountain above the timberline and evacuated its ranger station on Pine Creek, dangerously situated in the path of an old volcanic mudflow south of the mountain. As the Forest Service employees were leaving, geologists with metal suitcases packed with equipment were on their way in. The ground quivered beneath their feet.

Still, the mountain was barely news. Then on Thursday, March 27, Mike Beard, a traffic spotter for Portland radio station KGW, flew close to the mountain, hoping to get a fresh story idea. He found one. Near the summit, Beard saw steam and black ash spewing from a hole in the snow. "Hey, this thing's exploding!" he radioed back to his station. "There is no doubt the eruption is starting. You can see ash very, very clearly against the snow."

A black plume of steam and ash, hidden from those on the ground by overcast skies, shot 7,000 feet above the summit. When the plume subsided and

On March 27, after a week of subterranean shuddering, a loud boom resounded from the mountain at 12:36 p.m., and a plume of ash-laden steam exploded 7,000 feet into the sky. It was the first of hundreds of preliminary blasts that continued through the month of April (*right and inset*), titillating volcano-watchers and prompting dire warnings from USGS volcanologists. The dark ash, most of which was carried eastward by prevailing winds, stained the normally pure-white flanks of the mountain a malevolent black, giving the mountain an ominous two-toned appearance (*above*).

the clouds cleared, aerial observers saw that a new crater, 200 feet in diameter and 150 feet deep, had opened on top of the mountain. A dark smudge of volcanic ash blackened the snow and ice around the crater. Cracks up to three miles long ran east and west near the summit, indicating the north side of the peak had begun to slump.

Mount St. Helens was on the front pages of newspapers across the country the next morning and stayed there for more than two months. The news that Mount St. Helens was stirring and could be about to burst into a major eruption brought about a curious mass reaction: People were overjoyed. Washington Governor Dixy Lee Ray, a scientist herself, remarked to the press, "I've always said for many years that I hoped to live long enough to see one of our volcanoes erupt."

Sightseers rushed to the mountain, desperate to share in the excitement. The little towns around the base of the mountain—Cougar, Toutle, and Randle—were inundated with volcano-watchers. On Sunday, March 30, the mountain put on a spectacular show for them: 93 small eruptions of steam and ash spurted from the summit during the day. Traffic on Interstate 5 stopped, jamming the main route between Portland and Seattle.

Overhead, the sky buzzed with the engines of private planes and helicopters. The Federal Aviation Administration established a five-mile restricted zone around the mountain, but so many pilots disobeyed the order that, as one of them put it, "It's like a dogfight up there." On March 30 alone, according to the FAA, 70 unauthorized planes violated the airspace restrictions over the mountain.

With the bursts of ash rose a seemingly limitless entrepreneurial spirit. Mount St. Helens T-shirt hawkers made the rounds of the best viewing points, coming up with slogans like "Mount St. Helens is Hot!" or the premature "I Survived Mount St. Helens," and a wide variety of puns on the word "ash"—"Mount St. Helens ... Keep Your Ash Out of My Backyard." Enterprising salespeople collected samples of the volcanic ash that came gently drifting down like talcum powder, packaged it in glass vials or plastic baggies, and sold them as souvenirs.

In April, when seismometers began recording spasms of harmonic tremor, a type of continuous, rhythmic shaking that usually indicates magma moving beneath the earth's surface, the geologists' predictions grew increasingly grim. "This is like standing next to a dynamite keg and the fuse is lit, but you don't know how long the fuse is," Johnston told reporters gathered near the mountain. "If it exploded we would die."

David Johnston holds an impromptu press conference at the timberline parking lot on the north side of Mount St. Helens, March 27, 1980. It was here that Johnston referred to Mount St. Helens as a "dynamite keg" that could erupt at any time.

USGS geologist Don Swanson, an expert in measuring volcanic deformation, was dispatched to Washington state from the USGS Western Region Headquarters in Menlo Park immediately after the initial seismic activity in March 1980. He began taking detailed measurements of the mountain with the hope of predicting what the volcano might do next.

Even so, fear seemed to be the last thing on anyone's mind. Schoolchildren in Kelso wrote songs about the volcano. One went:

Let's get the lava flowing;
It's time to light the sky.
Let's get those ashes blowing
On Mount St. Helens tonight.
Boom! Boom! Boom! Boom!

Many people regarded the idea of an eruption as a joke; evading the roadblocks was a game. "I wish it would really do a big Pompeii bit on us," one excited volcano-watcher in Cougar told a newspaper reporter.

"People went over, under, through, and around every time we tried to restrict access to what we believed were dangerous areas," Skamania County Sheriff William Closner said. "There were even maps sold showing how to get around our blockades on the mountain. People were climbing right up to the rim of the crater. It would have taken the U.S. Army to control those people."

During the last weeks of April and early May, the mile-high bursts of steam and ash that had been shooting out of the top of the mountain stopped, delighting skeptics who had been pooh-poohing the whole thing, and frustrating reporters assigned to the volcano beat. The reporters' refrain, "We don't know when or if it's going to happen, but it could be any day now," grew less and less convincing. Desperate for stories, they interviewed volcano groupies. They did stories on geological history. They speculated on the volatility of other Cascade peaks. A reporter for *The Oregonian* in Portland called up 80-year-old Charles Richter, inventor of the Richter scale, at his home in Altadena, California, and asked for his prognosis on Mount St. Helens. Richter said he had no idea.

Harry Truman, a crotchety octogenarian who ran the Mount St. Helens Lodge in the shadow of the volcano, refused to leave his home at the base of the mountain and thereby became a media star. With his 16 cats, his pink Cadillac Coupe de Ville, and his Schenley bourbon, he was so perfect for the role it was as if he had been sent by a casting agency. Emboldened by the lull in activity, the National Geographic Society landed a helicopter on the mountain and took pictures. Days later, a Seattle film crew landed on the summit, filmed a beer commercial with the dark, steaming crater in the background, packed up, and flew away.

Most frustrated were the 100 or so people who owned vacation cabins in the vicinity of Spirit Lake. Governor Ray had established a "Red Zone" around the area, declaring it off-limits, and steadfastly refused to let the property owners back inside to fetch their belongings. The governor was unmoved by stories of starving cats, expensive cameras, and heirlooms left behind.

In early May, the angry property owners staged a protest at the Spirit Lake roadblock. They demanded permission to enter the restricted zone; some threatened to force their way in with guns. "We're going through that gate come hell or high water," one of the protestors, Chuck Williams, warned sheriff's deputies.

Fearing violence, Governor Ray relented—provided that the property owners sign waivers absolving the state of any responsibility for their welfare. On May 17, the day before the catastrophic eruption that buried Spirit Lake and all the cabins under 300 feet of mud and rock, a caravan of 20 property owners, many of them wearing T-shirts that said, "I own a piece of the rock," proceeded in a line up the highway to the lake. They were accompanied by a phalanx of reporters and photographers and led by a Washington State Patrol airplane. National Guard helicopters stood by for emergency evacuation. Four hours later, the property owners drove back down the valley, their backseats loaded with sheets and blankets, toasters, photographs, and radios. A second caravan was scheduled for ten o'clock the following morning—May 18.

During those weeks of outward calm, there was, in fact, significant activity going on beneath the surface. David Johnston and other geologists monitoring the shape of the mountain with laser beams noticed Mount St. Helens was growing—growing very quickly. Measurements in late April had shown an ominous bulge high on the north flank of the volcano that was increasing at a rate of five feet per day. Sections of the bulge were more than 450 feet higher than they had been weeks before, an indication that pressurized magma was being forced up through cracks and fissures in the mountain.

And then Mount St. Helens exploded.

Eleven seconds after 8:32 a.m. on May 18, as Gary Rosenquist squeezed the shutter of his camera on the ridge at Bear Meadow, a magnitude 5.1 earthquake a mile below the mountain shook the bulge loose. Weakened by the intrusion of magma and pressurized gases, Mount St. Helens literally collapsed on itself. The entire north half of the mountain slid downhill in the largest avalanche in recorded history.

Above: Private logging companies, reluctant to halt their lucrative timber-cutting operations in forests surrounding the awakening volcano, equipped their workers with devices to measure the ash content of the air. The loggers continued working, keeping a wary eye on the steaming mountain above them. The fact that the volcano erupted on a Sunday, the loggers' day off, saved hundreds of lives. *Right:* The irascible Harry Truman, 83-year-old owner and operator of the Mount St. Helens Lodge, scoffed at the idea that Mount St. Helens might blow up. He refused to leave his home on Spirit Lake despite official orders to evacuate. "That mountain will never hurt me," he said. "When you live someplace for 50 years, you either know your country or you're stupid."

Overleaf: Mount St. Helens bursts into spectacular eruption, May 18, 8:32 a.m.

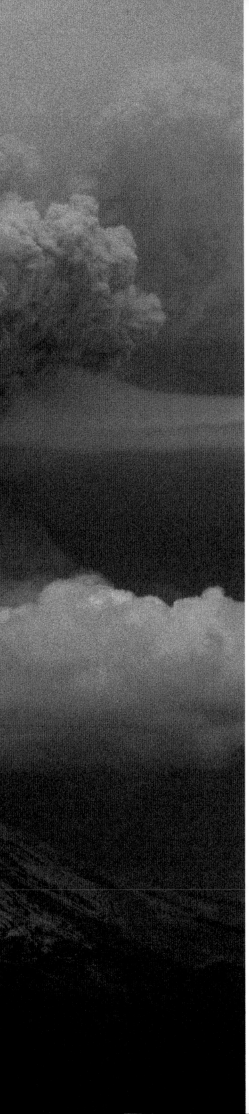

Rather than exploding straight up, the May 18 eruption burst laterally from the north side of the volcano, spreading destruction farther than even the most pessimistic projections. The heat and ash claimed many victims in areas generally assumed to be safe. Vancouver *Columbian* photographer Reid Blackburn witnessed the blast from eight miles away and, after firing off four frames, retreated to his car for protection. Two days later, a rescue team found his body inside the car (*inset, top*) nearly buried in ash and with the windows broken out. *Inset, bottom:* Nine miles away from the mountain, an abandoned van at ravaged Meta Lake.

At that moment, geologists Keith and Dorothy Stoffel were flying over the mountain's summit in a four-seat Cessna. "Within a matter of seconds, perhaps 15 seconds, the whole north side of the summit crater began to move instantaneously," Keith Stoffel reported later. "The nature of movement was eerie. The entire mass began to ripple and churn up, without moving laterally. Then the entire north side of the summit began sliding to the north along a deep-seated slide plane. We were amazed and excited with the realization that we were watching this landslide of unbelievable proportions. We took pictures of this slide sequence occurring, but before we could snap off more than a few pictures, a huge explosion blasted out. . . . We neither felt nor heard a thing, even though we were just east of the summit at this time."

With the plumes of the explosion blooming in the sky above them, the Stoffels' pilot put the Cessna into a steep dive and gave it full throttle, trying to outrun the cloud. Seconds before being engulfed, the tiny plane broke free and landed safely at Portland International Airport.

Instead of exploding straight up through the summit, the pent-up pressure blasted through the north side of the mountain, sending a blizzard of rock, ash, and hunks of glacial ice northward with a velocity that approached the speed of sound. A black cloud poured out of the mountain, hugging the ground as it rolled over ridges and churned down valleys. The lateral blast pulverized, incinerated, or blew away virtually everything in a fan-shaped swath of destruction that extended as far as 17 miles from the crater.

The noise of the explosion was heard as far away as Saskatchewan, and shock waves were clearly felt throughout the Puget Sound area, where many people described the impacts as "whumps." Windows rattled 100 miles away. Dishes fell from shelves; cracks opened in masonry walls. A vertical plume rose 16 miles into the atmosphere and continued unabated for nine hours.

The degrees of destruction spread northward in roughly concentric circles, beginning at the center of the volcano. In the "inner blast zone," within a few miles of the crater, the explosion vaporized every living thing. The force of the blast was so great that in places it stripped the soil from the underlying rock. Coldwater Ridge, six miles from the crater and directly in line with the blast, had been thickly forested before the eruption. Afterward, it was sandblasted to bare rock.

Geologist Johnston, who had been camping out on the top of the ridge, at the USGS Coldwater II observation station, barely had time to radio in one

The Sound of Silence

The force of Mount St. Helens's climactic outburst was equivalent to that of thousands of atomic bombs, yet, oddly, those closest to the volcano heard no sound of the explosion. Hikers and climbers on nearby Mount Adams, Mount Hood, and Mount Rainier watched the mountain disintegrate in eerie silence. Geologist Don Swanson, in a helicopter hovering alongside the eruptive column, compared the experience to watching a silent movie—"All that was missing was the tinkling piano." The closest observer in the blast zone who lived to tell his story was nine miles away; he reported hearing the thrashing and snapping of trees, but no sound of the explosion itself.

Meanwhile, people in the metropolitan areas of Seattle and Vancouver, British Columbia, were startled by a series of very loud bangs, which many compared to the sound of heavy artillery fired a short distance away. Residents along the Oregon coast thought they were hearing sonic booms, thunder, and dynamiting all rolled into one 15-minute barrage. The sound was heard as far away as the Canadian town of Maple Creek, Saskatchewan, 690 miles from the mountain.

Intrigued by the disparity, Clara Fairfield, curator at the Oregon Museum of Science and Industry in Portland, and John Dewey, physics professor at the University of Victoria in British Columbia, independently solicited responses from residents throughout the Pacific Northwest in the summer of 1980, asking people whether or not they had heard the eruption and, if so, what it had sounded like. On the basis of more than 5,200 responses, the scientists concluded that Mount St. Helens had been wrapped in a zone of silence that extended approximately 60 miles in every direction.

According to Dewey, the phenomenon occurs because sound waves travel faster in warmer air and tend to be refracted toward cooler temperatures. The sound waves that radiated out of the volcano were bent upward, toward cooler air at higher altitudes. At a distance of about 15 miles above the surface of the earth, in the middle levels of the stratosphere, the air temperatures begin to rise again from the radiant energy of the sun. When the sound waves reached this blanket of warmer air, they were refracted back down toward the surface of the earth, roughly in the shape of a flattened doughnut. The sound apparently bounced back and forth between the earth and the upper atmosphere a number of times, resulting in alternating zones of loudness and quiet at increasing distances from the volcano.

That much is fairly straightforward physics. The phenomenon of the zone of silence and the long-distance travel of sound has been recognized since World War I, when gunfire from the Western Front was heard as far away as London. What is more puzzling is that many people reported hearing not one explosion on the morning of May 18, but a series of them, separated by a few seconds. "We're not sure about that," Dewey says. "It could be that different pulses of sound emanated from the volcano, or possibly refraction took place at different levels in the stratosphere. There are still some uncertainties involved."

final report before he, his Jeep, his 22-foot trailer, and his monitoring equipment were swept away, never to be found. Johnston's final geological observation was perhaps the shortest of his career, but it could not have been more accurate: "Vancouver, Vancouver, this is it!" he shouted into his radio.

Harry Truman was dead, too—buried under 300 feet of avalanche debris. So was Reid Blackburn, a Vancouver *Columbian* photographer under contract to the USGS and *National Geographic*, stationed at Coldwater I observation station, two miles northwest of Johnston's station.

Beyond the inner blast zone, the trees were not disintegrated but were flash-burned and knocked down. In what came to be known as the "blowdown zone," all the trees—4.7 billion board feet of Douglas fir, cedar, and hemlock—on 86,600 acres were mowed down like tall grass. The tree trunks, some of them 500 years old and 7 feet in diameter, stayed where they landed, combed into swirls and eddies by the volcanic winds.

Outside the blowdown zone, at about 14 to 17 miles from the crater, the blast was hot enough to kill the trees but not strong enough to uproot them or break them off. There, in the "scorch zone," they remained standing, their branches shriveled and curled into delicate fleurs-de-lis.

The unexpected power of the eruption and the fact that it fired off sideways left emergency crews in utter confusion. The problems of the blast itself were compounded by waves of mud that came boiling down the mountain, and by the near-total lack of visibility caused by the airborne ash.

The intense heat of the eruption melted 70 percent of the snow and glaciers on the mountain. The water rushed down the steep slopes, combining with ash and avalanche debris to form a superheated slurry that moved at speeds of up to 80 miles an hour. The mudflows swept down several different drainages, but by far the largest and most destructive were those that tore into the upper tributaries of the Toutle River, northwest of the crater.

Picking up trees, boulders, houses, and logging trucks as it went, the mud roared into the north and south forks of the river, raising the water level of the Toutle by as much as 66 feet in places. The mud sloshed 360 feet up onto the sides of valleys and rolled over hills 250 feet high. Eight of the ten bridges across the river were jerked from their foundations or destroyed, and 37 miles of the Spirit Lake Highway were either buried or washed out. The cabins and farms in the lower Toutle River valley, some as far as 40 miles away from the mountain, were buried to their roofs. Hot mud oozed through living rooms and over vehicles like an ocean of wet concrete. At least 200 homes along the south and north forks of the river were either washed away,

Left: Superheated air at the leading edge of the blast, estimated at up to 480 degrees, killed millions of Douglas fir, hemlock, and cedar trees in a "scorch zone" surrounding the devastated area, leaving the trees standing but shriveling branches into ornate curls. *Inset:* In protected areas, such as behind ridges, trees were often snapped off but not uprooted. Here, in the lee of the crater wall, the forest was reduced to a stubble of shattered trunks. *Below:* More than 12 million board feet of timber stockpiled at three Weyerhaeuser Company logging camps were swept down the Toutle River by floods of melted snow and ice, wiping out eight bridges on the way to the Cowlitz and Columbia rivers. *Overleaf:* Seventy percent of the ice and snow stored on Mount St. Helens turned to water in the eruption, causing disastrous flooding in the Toutle River valley. At least 200 homes along the Toutle were washed away, buried in mud, or otherwise damaged.

buried, or otherwise damaged. More than 1,000 people were evacuated. At noon, when the first wave of mud reached the Cowlitz River, 45 miles away, it was so hot that it raised the water temperature to 90 degrees. Salmon leaped out of the river to avoid the heat.

In all, more than 100 million cubic yards of sediment were deposited along the lower Cowlitz and Columbia rivers. The water-carrying capacity of the Cowlitz was reduced by 85 percent, and the depth of the navigational channel in the Columbia decreased from 39 feet to less than 13 feet for a distance of two miles, shutting down ocean shipping. Thirty-one vessels were stranded in the ports of Portland, Vancouver, and Kalama.

Along with its load of 12 million board feet of timber, the Toutle River flood swept untold numbers of horses, sheep, cattle, and millions of fish to their deaths.

While to the west side of the mountain there was mud to contend with, the east side was confronted with a different horror: ash. When Mount St. Helens erupted, it shot a vertical column of pulverized rock 15 miles into the atmosphere in 15 minutes. It continued to pump out ash for nine hours, producing a black cloud that held somewhere between 1.7 and 2.4 billion cubic yards of material. Lightning created by colliding ash particles flashed around the edges of the cloud. Prevailing winds carried it to the north and east, dumping fine, gritty material that ranged in consistency from flour to beach sand over wheat fields in the Columbia Basin and orchards in the Yakima Valley, where some fruit trees were in blossom.

Above and inset: Slurries of mud surged down the north and south forks of the Toutle River, mangling trucks, scattering logging equipment, and sweeping away trees, buildings, automobiles, and miles of roads. *Right:* At the Weyerhaeuser Company's 12-Road logging camp on the South Fork of the Toutle River, 22 miles from the mountain, trucks were tossed like toys, and ruptured storage tanks oozed chemicals. At three Weyerhaeuser logging camps damaged by mudflows, the company lost a total of 30 logging trucks, 22 crew buses, and 39 railroad cars. *Below:* A river of logs flowed down the Toutle, into the Cowlitz River, and on to the Columbia River.

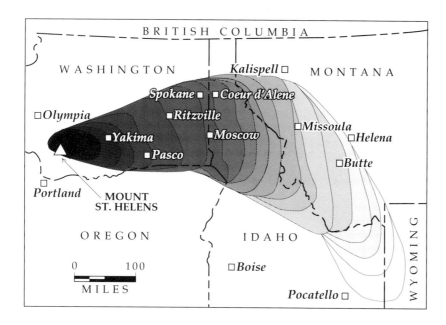

Above: During the first nine hours of the eruption, the volcano spewed out 540 million tons of ash, which fell over an area of more than 22,000 square miles. The densest part of the cloud traveled downwind in the pattern superimposed on the above map. Each concentric circle within the cloud indicates one-half hour of elapsed time.

Within three hours the plume had totally blocked the sun over half the state. Light-activated streetlamps flickered on in Spokane and Yakima before noon on the day of the eruption, thereafter known as Ash Sunday. Traveling quickly on the wind, the cloud darkened Idaho, then Montana. It arrived in Boston in two days, and in 17 days had completely encircled the globe, appearing once again over the West Coast.

On Eastern Washington highways, the ash clogged the air filters of car and truck engines, leaving some 5,000 motorists stranded. Two days after the eruption, Governor Ray announced that more than half of the vehicles operated by police and emergency services were out of commission.

In some respects the dry ash was like snow—except it did not melt. When it got wet, it took on the consistency of cement. Ash closed virtually every major highway in Eastern Washington. Airplanes were grounded, trains halted, truck traffic stopped. In Spokane, work crews removed 100,000 tons of ash from the Spokane International Airport. In the town of Ritzville, 195 miles from the mountain, atmospheric idiosyncrasies caused ash to fall from the sky as if from a demonic backhoe. Fine grey ash the consistency of talcum powder lay four inches thick on roadways and lawns, and collected in drifts three feet high. More than 2,000 travelers were stranded in Ritzville on May 18, doubling the town's population for three days. People slept on church pews and gymnasium floors and in a cafe converted to a shelter. On May 21, when the roads were at last clear enough to drive, sheriff's deputies led a caravan of 1,500 drivers out of town, a giant rooster tail of ash flying up behind them.

One of the chief concerns of people in Eastern Washington was the long-term health effect of breathing the ash. At Washington State University in Pullman, 3,358 students dropped out before the end of the term, worrying

Above: President Jimmy Carter, who flew to Washington state three days after the eruption, chats with radio operators at the volcano communications center in Vancouver. Carter inspected the devastated area on May 23 and remarked, "It makes the surface of the moon look like a golf course." *Left:* Residents of Spokane, worried about the health effects of inhaling the abrasive ash, take emergency measures to clear the air.

about a lung ailment few could pronounce: pneumonoultramicroscopicsilicovolcanoconiosis. People appeared on the streets of east-side cities with their faces wrapped in rags or wearing industrial face masks. A chronic shortage of the masks developed, and paper coffee filters were used instead. President Carter, who flew into the state for a tour of the disaster area, promised that two million face masks would be sent immediately. The Minnesota Mining & Manufacturing Company—3M—sent its entire inventory of one million masks to the Northwest.

Meanwhile, as rescuers picked through the hot ash and downed trees in the devastated area, the number of human victims grew steadily. *The Oregonian* reported nine dead the day after the blast. As missing-person reports came in, it became clear that the actual number of those who had died would be several times higher than that. The official total took two years to determine and is now clicked off along with the rest of the eruption statistics: board feet of timber destroyed: 4.7 billion; number of feet the mountain was reduced in height: 1,313; height of the ash plume: 16 miles; persons killed: 57.

Autopsies of 25 victims of the blast—their bodies so saturated with ash that inch-deep incisions dulled scalpel blades—indicated that most died of suffocation by inhalation of volcanic ash. The gritty ash mixed with mucous and plugged their throats and noses. Doctors at the universities of Washington and Oregon reported that the victims' hands were mummified; muscles appeared dried and frayed, and internal organs had shrunk and hardened. Those who suffocated died within minutes, the researchers said, while some of those who were burned survived long enough to walk several miles for help.

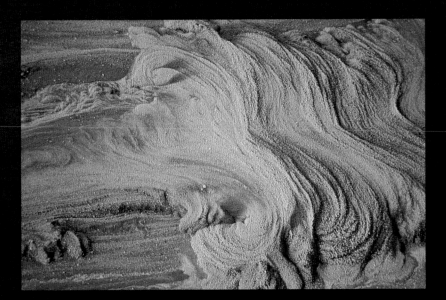

Preceding page: The ash turned day into night in much of Central and Eastern Washington, activating light-sensitive street lamps in mid-afternoon in Ellensburg and billowing over Ephrata, 145 miles from the peak, three hours after the eruption (*inset, top*). Powdery ash blanketed fertile agricultural land in the Palouse region of Eastern Washington (*inset, middle*), smothering fields of sprouting wheat and sculpting ornate patterns when wet (*inset, bottom*). *Right:* Safely out of harm's way, a family north of Vancouver contemplates the apocalyptic spectacle of ascending ash.

Nearly two hundred people caught in the blast made it out alive, most of them airlifted to safety aboard National Guard helicopters. The youngest survivor, three-month-old Terra Moore of Castle Rock, was trapped with her family in the ash for two days at their campsite near the Green River before they were rescued. Twenty-seven bodies were never found, and there are those who still insist the number of dead is actually higher than the official count.

Some of the victims died purely because of bad luck, others out of ignorance or because of misinformation. "I just thought some little puffs of smoke would come out and the lava would dribble down," said a survivor. One couple was killed as they watched the eruption from a viewpoint 25 miles away.

But most died seeking the sheer excitement of it all. Search crews found some victims still clutching cameras, exemplifying human characteristics that, for better or worse, set the human species apart from all others: stubbornness so entrenched that it defies all common sense, and curiosity so consuming that it continues to the very abyss.

THE ANATOMY OF A VOLCANO

Don Swanson is never quite sure how to react when people call him "Mr. Crater." And it's true that when his colleagues at the U.S. Geological Survey or the University of Washington refer to him that way, it can sound slightly sarcastic. But the title was bestowed on Swanson with the best of faith. It amounts to recognition, pure and simple, that he knows more about the burned-out crater of Mount St. Helens than any other geologist.

Swanson has studied a number of other volcanoes around the world. His particular field of research—analyzing the movements that mountains tend to make before they burst into eruption—has taken him to Italy, the Canary Islands, Japan, and New Zealand. But Mount St. Helens has captured Swanson's imagination in a way no other volcano has. He has spent the better part of his career with it—watching, probing, and analyzing its moods. He camps next to it; he climbs around in the fumaroles (gas vents) steaming on its dome; in the winter he burrows through the snow to get to instruments stashed on the crater floor.

Swanson's relationship with Mount St. Helens began on camping trips when he was growing up in Centralia, Washington, in the 1940s and 1950s. He first saw the mountain professionally in 1972, when he took detailed measurements of it for the USGS. When the first blast of steam and ash erupted from the mountain on March 27, 1980, the 41-year-old Swanson was put in charge of one of the teams monitoring the volcano. He arrived in Vancouver, Washington, at approximately the same time as five others in the USGS elite corps of volcano specialists: Cascade-Range experts Donal Mullineaux and Dwight "Rocky" Crandell, Robert Christiansen, Jim Moore, and the agency's rising star, David Johnston. In the weeks before the eruption, the six geologists attended the mountain like obstetricians at a difficult birth. They took its subterranean pulse, analyzed its every exhalation, and watched anxiously as a tumorous growth ballooned out of its north side.

After Mount St. Helens's violent outburst on May 18, Swanson lobbied strenuously—and successfully—for the right to work directly inside the crater, arguing that the scientific value of the evidence there outweighed any possible risks to his life or to government equipment. He has continued to scrutinize the mountain in the years since then, working out of the USGS Cascades Volcano Observatory in Vancouver. Swanson is by no means the only geologist studying the mountain. Some 20 other geologists at the observatory devote most of their time to Mount St. Helens. But now that Crandell and Mullineaux have retired, Swanson is the grand old man of the group.

Wisps of vented steam rise from the hollowed-out crater of Mount St. Helens, with Mount Adams in the distance. *Inset:* Geologist Don Swanson at the base of the new lava dome inside the crater. **59**

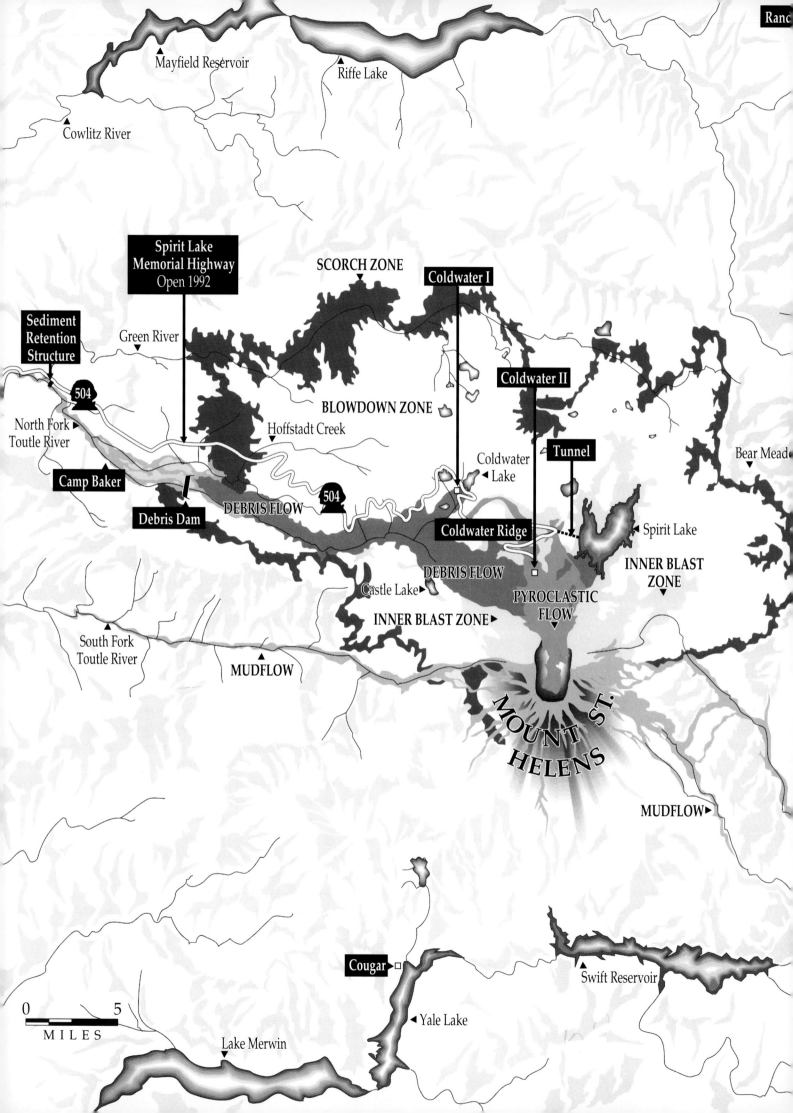

Mayfield Reservoir

Riffe Lake

Cowlitz River

Spirit Lake
Memorial Highway
Open 1992

SCORCH ZONE

Coldwater I

Sediment
Retention
Structure

Green River

Coldwater II

504

BLOWDOWN ZONE

Coldwater
Lake

Tunnel

North Fork
Toutle River

Hoffstadt Creek

Camp Baker

504

Coldwater Ridge

Bear Mead

Debris Dam

DEBRIS FLOW

Spirit Lake

DEBRIS FLOW

INNER BLAST
ZONE

Castle Lake

PYROCLASTIC
FLOW

South Fork
Toutle River

INNER BLAST ZONE ▶

MUDFLOW

MOUNT ST.
HELENS

MUDFLOW ▶

Cougar

Swift Reservoir

0   5

MILES

Yale Lake

Lake Merwin

Volcanologists studying Mount St. Helens have refined techniques of predicting volcanic activity, but the seismometer (*above*) is still one of their most basic and reliable tools. *Overleaf:* The new lava dome inside the crater proved to be an invaluable working model, providing geologists with repeated opportunities for testing theories and refining data as the dome grew in fits and starts over a period of six years.

Mount St. Helens turned out to be an almost ideal model for studying how volcanoes work. Not only is it easily accessible, but after its devastating eruption in 1980, it obligingly continued erupting in a modest way for ten years. During 1980, explosive eruptions occurred on May 25, June 12, July 22, August 7, and October 16, 17, and 18, producing ash columns that rose as high as 50,000 feet above sea level and pyroclastic flows (hot, dry bursts of pumice and ash) that extended as far as five miles north of the crater. After the June eruption, a batch of thick, pasty lava oozed out of the vent and formed a 140-foot-high dome on the crater floor. That dome and the beginnings of two subsequent ones were destroyed in later eruptions. A lava dome that formed after the October 1980 eruption remained in place and grew larger with each extrusion of lava. All eruptions and dome-building events that occurred between 1980 and 1990 were closely monitored by geologists, providing them with plenty of opportunities to test new theories and refine data.

The discoveries Swanson and his colleagues have made in the process of monitoring Mount St. Helens have changed the world of volcanology. Their findings have influenced how prehistoric volcanic deposits are interpreted and refined the science of predicting volcanic hazards.

Swanson has another, more personal connection with Mount St. Helens. On May 17, 1980, the day before the mountain exploded, it was his turn to man the USGS observation post on Coldwater Ridge, the station closest to the volcanic vent. Geologists were going to take turns sleeping in the USGS trailer parked there and use laser beams to measure the growing bulge on the north side of the mountain. Swanson, who was David Johnston's immediate supervisor at the time, had a friend visiting from Germany and wanted to take him to the airport Sunday morning. He asked Johnston to consider trading shifts with him.

Johnston didn't want to. He had other things going on, and he felt uncharacteristically nervous about spending the night so close to the volcano. Swanson was persuasive. Johnston reluctantly agreed.

Early Sunday morning, the mountain let loose with a powerful sideways blast aimed directly at Coldwater Ridge. The force of the explosion was so great that it scoured the top of the ridge down to solid bedrock. David Johnston's body was never found.

This is not a story Swanson tells often or easily. It's not that he feels responsible for Johnston's death or guilty for not having been in his place. He is too much of a scientist for that, too much aware of the general randomness of events in the universe. But the two men were close. "What I felt was a responsibility to do my job as well as it could be done," Swanson says. "Maybe partly for him."

Swanson and his colleagues arrived at Mount St. Helens in March 1980 with a strong basis of knowledge about how volcanoes in the Cascade Mountains work. By then the concept of plate tectonics, regarded as a theory from deep in right field as recently as the late 1960s, had become accepted by most American scientists.

That model of global physics, the rudiments of which were first proposed by German meteorologist Alfred L. Wegener in 1912, holds that the outer crust of the planet is composed of individual plates, floating on the molten core of the earth like fat on cold turkey soup. The plates are in constant motion, responding to the heat of the roiling cauldron below them. As the plates move, they crunch and grind against one another, providing the energy that fuels the world's earthquakes and volcanoes.

The sliding action between plates manifests itself as earthquakes. When one plate takes the path of least resistance and dives below the other, a process geologists call subduction, the pressure is so intense that the edges of the plate melt into magma. Because of the magma's relatively low density and resulting buoyance, it makes its way to the surface through weak spots in the earth's crust. When the magma hits the top, it spews out onto the surface: Voila! Volcanoes.

Wegener's basic theory had been sharpened considerably by the time Mount St. Helens erupted. Geologists had begun to understand that the plate under the Pacific Ocean, some 60 miles thick, is gradually expanding from rifts in its center. As the Pacific Plate spreads apart—at about the rate at which fingernails grow—it forces its edges into the continents that surround it, from New Zealand north through Japan, Russia to Alaska, and on down the west coasts of North and South America. This so-called "Ring of Fire" accounts for more than three-quarters of the 1,343 volcanoes in the world that are believed to have been active in the past 10,000 years.

Along the west coast of North America, the Pacific Plate bumps and grinds along the edge of the North American Plate, an uneasy relationship that shows up as California's San Andreas Fault. In the Pacific Northwest, the interaction among plates is more complicated. About a hundred or so miles off the Northwest coast is a smaller spreading area from which a smaller plate expands. This smaller plate, the Juan de Fuca, is expanding directly toward the North American Plate rather than slipping along beside it as the Pacific Plate does. At the junction between the two, the Juan de Fuca Plate dives below the North American Plate and, at a depth of about 100 miles, begins to melt, providing the molten rock and gases that come bubbling up beneath the Cascade Range.

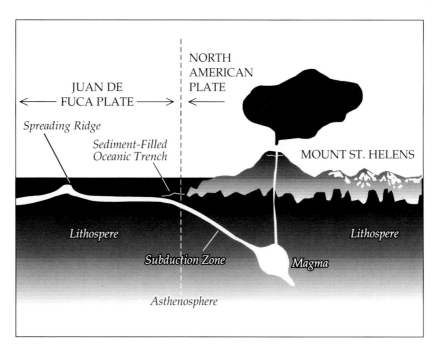

Above: Most geologists now attribute volcanic activity in the Cascade Range to the movement of "plates" on the surface of the earth. The relatively small Juan de Fuca Plate is forced under the larger North American Plate, creating such heat and pressure that molten rock rises to the surface through weak spots in the crust. *Left:* Ash rises above the clouds during one of several pulses of eruptions on July 22, 1980.

For 50 million years or so, the Cascades and much of Oregon and Washington to the east have spewed out lava that has ranged in consistency from molasses to popcorn. The largest flows took place about 15 million years ago when some 35,000 cubic miles of liquid basalt gushed forth from long cracks, or fissures, in the earth and, flowing at about the pace of a fast sprinter, flooded most of Eastern Washington and Eastern Oregon.

More recently, the magma oozing up under the Cascades has not been basalt, which tends to be fluid and stable, but more viscous—explosive batches of rock called andesite and dacite. In these more violent eruptions, the lava typically blasts out with enormous force, sending huge columns of pulverized lava, or ash, into the air and piling up burned-out cinders around the vent. Volcanoes formed this way, as Mount St. Helens and the rest of the Cascade peaks were, are called stratovolcanoes. The Cascade volcanoes, spread out for 700 miles from Lassen Peak in Northern California to Mount Garibaldi in southern British Columbia, are basically piles of volcanic rubble, strengthened periodically by magma that seeps into the voids and hardens. During the past 10,000 years, the Cascade volcanoes have produced at least one major eruption per century.

Some of the other volcanoes in the range have erupted with far greater force than Mount St. Helens. When the ancient Mount Mazama in Oregon erupted about 7,000 years ago, it blew out 42 times the ash and enough fresh lava to build two mountains the size of Mount St. Helens. Mazama collapsed into itself after its climactic blast, forming what is now Crater Lake.

When Don Swanson arrived at Mount St. Helens in 1980, all of these basics of volcanology were well established. With the exception of the revolutionary concept of plate tectonics, he had studied most of them in geology courses at Washington State University and later at Johns Hopkins University, where he took his Ph.D. Far more pertinent to the emergency at hand was a report specifically about Mount St. Helens that Mullineaux and Crandell had written in 1978. The two geologists had been studying strato-volcanoes in the Cascade Range since the early 1960s, prowling around the mountains' slopes and the surrounding forest land, poking into old mudflows and peering at road cuts to trace sedimentary layering.

In 1978, Mullineaux and Crandell published a detailed study of Mount St. Helens, outlining its particular history and hazards. The mountain was very young, Mullineaux and Crandell noted, most of it having risen like a loaf of bread in the past 2,000 years or so. The reason for the volcano's almost perfectly conical shape was that it hadn't yet been carved by weather and glaciers, as had the nearby peaks of Mount Rainier, Mount Adams, and Mount Hood. But Mount St. Helens had been built on top of a much older volcano that had been active for at least 40,000 years. By carbon dating plant life buried in old debris flows, Mullineaux and Crandell found evidence of 23 major explosive eruptions of Mount St. Helens in the past 4,500 years—more than any other volcano in the coterminous United States. During one of Mount St. Helens's past eruptive periods, 3,000 to 4,000 years ago, the volcano had tossed out quantities of ash that today are distinguishable as a sedimentary layer in Alberta, Canada, 580 miles away.

The last period of eruptions of Mount St. Helens before 1980 took place between 1831 and 1857, during which a number of eyewitnesses reported billowy, ash-laden clouds, periods of darkness, and glowing skies.

Because of the mountain's stormy history, Mullineaux and Crandell predicted in 1975 that the volcano would erupt again soon—perhaps before the end of the century. And in their major 1978 report, titled "Potential Hazards from Future Eruptions of Mount St. Helens, Washington," they went further, describing St. Helens as "the volcano most likely to endanger people and property in the western United States." The predictions they made in that report, referred to alternatively by geologists working at the scene of the eruption as "the Blue Book" or "the Bible," proved to be remarkably close to what actually took place two years later. The shortfall of the report, however, was that it severely underplayed the possibility of a lateral blast and underestimated its potential power by a factor of three.

While the scientists had a good grasp of volcanic processes and a detailed personality analysis of Mount St. Helens in particular, what none of them knew—not Crandell, Mullineaux, Swanson, Johnston, or any of the

Above: The dome of extruded lava growing on the floor of the crater in April 1981 presents a remarkable contrast with the same view of the mountain one year earlier (*inset*), when the crater first began to open on the summit. Rapid changes are nothing new to Mount St. Helens. Geologists believe that most of the volcano's cone rose within the past 2,000 years, leading some to refer to it as "a mountain in a hurry."

others — were the mysterious techniques of mass communication. They were geologists, accustomed to spending long solitary hours in the field with their sample bags and rock hammers or in quiet offices, working out details of events that usually took hundreds of thousands of years to unfold and which concerned very few people. In Vancouver, where the Forest Service office quickly became the main information center for developing events on Mount St. Helens, the geologists were thrust into an atmosphere of potential panic.

Mullineaux, Crandell, and Steve Malone, the U.W. seismologist who first noted the telltale swarms of earthquakes under the volcano, suddenly became Isaiahs of the mountain, called on for prophecies day and night by nervous officials and hungry, aggressive reporters. What everyone wanted to know was what the scientists couldn't tell them: how big and when? The USGS experts had fairly detailed ideas about what might happen, but their predictions were heavily based in probability and had margins of error that stretched into months or even years.

As Mullineaux recalled later, "People wanted specific answers. Every time I told a press conference the volcano could go on for weeks, months, or years, or it could progress to a larger eruption, or it could stay the same, I saw the reporters just put their heads in their hands."

The pressure for information kept the scientists from doing their work. Crandell, for example, was too busy during the day to lay out a hazards map of the area so other agencies could establish danger zones around the mountain and evacuate people where necessary. The first map, Crandell later told sociologists studying the USGS response to the eruption, "I did between the hours of one and five one morning simply because it was not possible to do it in the daytime. Six telephones were ringing incessantly."

Swanson, better at dodging calls, was able to concentrate more on science. He spent every available minute in the field, setting up equipment to measure the shape of the volcano, either camping out at night or holing up in the Shilo Motel in Vancouver. The monitoring devices he and other geologists set up in the weeks preceding the blast made Mount St. Helens the best-documented volcanic eruption in history. By the time it exploded on May 18, Mount St. Helens had been intricately wired. Seismometers measured every lurch and tremor. Laser beams that bounced off targets on the mountain tracked changes in its size to the nearest millimeter. Samples of the gases wafting off its summit were collected and analyzed for sulphur dioxide content, an indicator of explosive activity. High-altitude surveillance planes and satellites took its temperature with infrared photography.

In retrospect, the sequence of events on May 18 seem perfectly logical: Rising magma inside the mountain pushed a bulge outward on its north flank (*far left*). The earthquake at 8:32 a.m. shook the unstable bulge loose, triggering an avalanche that depressurized magmatic gases (*middle*). The resulting explosion was at first channeled northward by the intact walls of the crater, then, with the top of the mountain out of the way, the eruptive column rose straight up, driven by a chain reaction of explosions that worked its way down into the mountain's core (*left*). Later, a new dome formed on the crater floor (*below*).

Still, Mount St. Helens fooled them all. When it exploded on May 18, it did so essentially without warning. More surprising, it let loose with a sideways blast more powerful than anyone had imagined possible.

The failure to predict what would happen left many of the geologists deeply disappointed. "There was a big sense of failure around here. We had missed it," Malone remembered. "And we had lost a friend [David Johnston]. Everyone was just thrown into a kind of a deep, dark depression for awhile."

After the ash had settled and the initial catastrophes sorted out, scientific attention focused on the particulars of what had been missed: the magnitude of the collapse and the direction of the blast. According to geological evidence, Mount St. Helens had never erupted with a big lateral explosion before, and therefore, the possibility was not seriously considered. That surprise brought about a basic change in the way volcanic hazards are assessed. As USGS geologist Richard Hoblitt put it, "Before 1980, the volcanic-hazards assessment for a given volcano in the Cascade Range were based on events that had previously occurred at that volcano. The 1980 directed blast showed that unprecedented events are possible and that they need to be considered."

What had happened was, in retrospect, completely logical. The magma had forced its way into the rocks and crevasses inside the volcano and begun prying the structure apart. The mountain, built mainly of loose rocks and rubble from previous eruptions, had little internal strength. The intruding magma pushed the structure to the limits of its stability. No one is sure what caused the triggering earthquake early Sunday morning, but its movement shook off the bulge of distended rock, which by then had shoved the north flank outward more than 300 feet. The mountain collapsed on itself. When that happened, it was as if a cork had been removed from a bottle of champagne. The superheated magma inside the mountain depressurized instantly and, as water in the magma flashed into steam, it literally blew the mountain to pieces. (When water changes from a liquid to a gaseous state, its volume increases 1,000 times.) As overlying rock exploded, it exposed fresh magma inside the mountain. The dissolved gases in the magma exploded in turn, blasting the rock to ash and exposing even more superheated magma below. Over the nine-hour course of the eruption, the series of explosions worked their way down into the core of the mountain.

The phenomenon of collapsing volcanoes had been recognized for some time, but until May 18, 1980, nobody had actually witnessed one in action. The Mount St. Helens avalanche and blast were not only photographed

from several angles on land and in the air, but were caught in infrared by two military satellites and recorded on at least a dozen seismographs. This gave scientists an excellent record of the symptoms that preceded the eruption and provided them with tangible evidence of the aftermath.

The distinctive lumpy deposits of rock, old lava flows, domes, and pyroclastic flows strewn out from the open mouth of the crater by the avalanche resembled others around the world that had previously mystified geologists. In Northern California's Shasta River valley, for example, geologists had been puzzling for 50 years over an area of strange mounds and small hills, trying to figure out what could have put them there. Some theorized they were small, individual volcanoes, others proposed that they had been left there by glaciers or carved out by streams.

The striking similarity of the Shasta River deposits to those left at the head of the Toutle River valley by Mount St. Helens led geologists to conclude that Shasta's mystery lumps were evidence of a similar collapsing volcano, 300,000 years ago. More than 100 other such deposits have been identified since then, from Socompa, a volcano in northern Chile, to Pelée in the West Indies, to the island of Molokai in Hawaii, half of which some geologists now believe was carried away in a Mount St. Helens-style landslide. Collapsing volcanoes, geologists have learned, are not at all rare.

Another stunning feature of the May 18 explosion was the size and destructive force of the slurries of mud that boiled down the mountain's slopes. Oceans of mud formed on the slopes of the volcano and, with a consistency of wet concrete, poured into surrounding river drainages with enough power to wrench concrete bridges from their footings, pick up entire railroad trestles, and sweep virtually everything in their path down the Toutle River valley.

The fact that volcanoes can cause mudflows was no revelation. Mudflows similar to those on Mount St. Helens are fairly common in eruptions in Indonesia and in scientific literature are referred to by their Indonesian name—lahars. The processes by which lahars are formed, however, and the physics of how they behave were not well understood.

After analyzing the well-documented evidence of what took place on Mount St. Helens, scientists were able to piece together a number of ways in which lahars originate. On Mount St. Helens, which had been covered with glacial ice and snow at the time of the eruption, the extreme heat of the emerging rock, estimated at between 700 and 1,000 degrees Fahrenheit, almost instantly turned 70 percent of the ice and snow on the upper slopes to

Left: Steam from groundwater contacting still-hot magma hisses out of fumaroles on the lava dome at a fairly constant rate, although the vapors are not always visible. When atmospheric conditions are right, the rim of the crater resembles a roiling cauldron (*inset*).

water. The hot water surged down the steep slopes, picking up the light ash and debris from the avalanche as it dropped—at speeds of up to 80 miles per hour.

The biggest lahar—the one that went down the North Fork Toutle in the afternoon and early evening—had a different origin altogether. It formed as the debris avalanche "dewatered" on the floor of the valley. The avalanche material carried water from several sources: snow and melting ice from the flanks of the volcano; water in the Toutle River; and water that sloshed out of Spirit Lake. The water was dispersed throughout the avalanche, and it took several hours for it to work its way to the surface as the material settled. Once water reached the surface, it began to flow. Gradually, it increased to a torrent that eroded the avalanche and finally rushed downstream as a lahar. "This was one of the most important things we learned about the May 18 events," Swanson says, "the importance of dewatering in generating quite a large lahar hours after things should have calmed down."

In subsequent activity on Mount St. Helens, smaller lahars were formed in a variety of other ways: heavy rain falling on easily eroded volcanic deposits, landslides, and, on occasion, lakes breaking out of their natural dams. By watching how these lahars behaved, geologists were able to discover clues about lahar physics—when lahars are likely to pick up additional rocks and soil, becoming more concentrated and destructive, for example, and when they are likely to drop solid material as they go, transforming themselves into floods.

By watching the landscape created by the mud and avalanche flows in the vicinity of Mount St. Helens, geologists came to realize that volcanic eruptions themselves are just the beginning of dramatic changes brought on by volcanoes. Immediately after the eruption, the base of the mountain and the river valleys dropping to the west were transformed into a deranged jumble of weirdly uniform, rounded hills. When the dust cleared, geologists were presented with a virgin landscape, untouched by erosion, and were able to watch it develop as if from the beginning of time, as natural forces brought it into equilibrium. They had the opportunity to watch the birth of rivers, waterfalls, lakes, and plateaus—evolutionary processes that normally stretch over millennia concentrated into a matter of months, or even days.

The process was most dramatic in the avalanche material and mudflows, where a single rain could mean the birth of new creeks and tributaries. At the head of the Toutle River valley, which had been plugged with a mountain

The eruption's devastating effects were just the beginnings of the dramatic changes the volcano made in the landscape. Inside the mountain (*above*) the bared crater walls are highly unstable, and rockfalls continually cascade down their sides. The crater floor (*right*) has undergone constant metamorphosis since 1980, changing form with the influences of water, avalanches, and extruded lava. In front of the crater on the pyroclastic flow (*inset*), water and wind are rapidly eroding to dust chunks of pumice that were once as large as automobiles.

of debris 14 miles long and as much as 600 feet deep, water erosion quickly carved deep chasms in the unstable material, creating brand new canyons that directed the water and snowmelt down the Toutle.

Inside the crater itself, avalanches constantly tumbled down the steep walls exposed by the blast, giving geologists a chance to observe the process by which mountains erode, compressed as if by time-lapse photography.

This world is Don Swanson's wonderland. Inside the crater, the geologic forces normally detectable only through rocks thousands of years old are alive and thrashing around. The crater fires up his imagination. It's a place where every expectation about nature is turned upside-down, where waterfalls are steaming hot, where the stream banks are unearthly shades of crimson and green with algae. It is as if a chunk of an alien planet, or an environment somehow transported through millions of years in time, were plopped down in the middle of the cool, green Pacific Northwest. For the uninitiated it is difficult not to see it as a premonition of the end of life on earth.

Swanson doesn't look at it that way. "Nature doesn't know words like 'desolation' and 'devastation,' " he says. "Sometimes I catch myself describing this area as 'devastated' or something like that, but I try not to. I look at this area here and see a real desertlike beauty to it. It's been said many times before, but it's true: The only thing permanent is change."

Inside the horseshoe-shaped crater, the lava dome has filled the floor to its edges. It's a craggy heap of brand-new rock, more than a half-mile wide and 1,150 feet high. Up close it looks like a mountain from Mars. Steam from a hundred fumaroles in its sides wafts up to join the clouds twisting and weeping overhead. The noise of rockfalls is constant, as the walls of old domes and lava flows exposed in the crater wall spatter down to the floor. In the natural amphitheater the noise is clear but has no direction; the falling rock sounds like applause, coming from everywhere at once. The crater walls erupt in brown puffs of dust as the rocks bounce down, as if strafed by invisible machine guns.

Above: Geologists were able to document the birth of new creeks as water cut into easily erodible volcanic deposits after the eruption. *Right:* A "breadcrust bomb," volcanic ejecta blown out of the crater while still semi-molten. Cracks on the surface of the "bomb" are caused by interior gases that continue expanding after the outer crust has cooled and solidified.

Shortly after the May 18 eruption, when the new dome began rising from the crater floor, many scientists predicted that in 200 years or so it would rise to fill the chasm left by the eruption. Swanson doesn't think that will be the case. Instead, he predicts that the old crater walls surrounding the dome will crumble to the crater floor and partially bury it—not a comforting thought for climbers who routinely ascend the crater's south face and peer over the unstable edge. "Fifty years from now the dome will look only half as high as now because of rockfalls," he says. "Gravity is a powerful agent."

The chief disappointment about the May 18 eruption of Mount St. Helens was that even though it was monitored to the technical limits of science, Swanson and other geologists on the scene were unable to give any short-term notice of what was to happen on the morning of May 18—not the timing, and not the intensity. Even with the best scientists and equipment, it was not possible to say, "Here it comes," in time to prevent the deaths of at least 57 people. In retrospect, the restricted area established around the mountain was far too small. If it had not been for the timing of the blast— early Sunday morning—the number of deaths would undoubtedly have been much higher. The Weyerhaeuser Company had 330 employees working in the area on weekdays.

For the perceived failure to predict the time and force of the blast, the USGS and other public agencies have been subject to criticism. Some relatives of victims of the eruption went so far to claim that the state intentionally withheld information from the public regarding the potential hazards and established restricted zones that were too small in order to allow continued logging by the Weyerhaeuser Company. The suits against the state were dismissed in 1985, when a judge ruled there was no evidence to support the claim and found that the governor's establishment of the

restricted zones — on the advice of federal experts — was entirely discretionary. To the USGS geologists, who helped establish the zones, the death of David Johnston at an observation site that was considered safe is an eloquent rebuttal of those charges.

While the failure to foresee the devastating eruption had undeniably tragic results, it was not surprising, considering how new the field of geological predictions is. Geologists are historians of the earth, not futurists. They entered into the field of predicting hazards of geological events less than 20 years ago with earthquakes and, despite a rapidly expanding base of knowledge, have never been able to predict an earthquake with enough accuracy to save lives or prevent property damage. And far less is known about volcanoes than earthquakes.

Since the eruption, a great deal of attention has been focused on sharpening the ability to predict volcanic hazards. While the specifics of the major activity on Mount St. Helens were missed, the unprecedented documentation of the event provided a number of clues that have made predictions easier. As a result of what has been learned, 17 dome-building eruptions at Mount St. Helens that occurred after May 18 were predicted from one to three weeks in advance — a feat unparalleled in volcanology.

The most basic tool for predicting volcanic eruptions has been the seismometer — a machine that records ways in which the earth tends to shudder and shake before the blasts. In the case of Mount St. Helens, seismologists had the mountain wired well before the first tremors. Prior to the initial quake March 20, the University of Washington had a single seismometer on the west flank of the volcano. Within 48 hours, Malone and others had installed three more seismic stations on the mountain; within 10 days, 13 new stations had been established. From that point on, analysts at the U.W. geophysics laboratory were able to correlate the zig-zags they saw on their printouts with what was actually happening on the mountain.

Geologists have been using seismic activity to predict volcanic eruptions for decades, but it has been a relatively crude tool. Seismic interpreters working with Mount St. Helens raised the techniques to new levels of sophistication. Like blind men examining an elephant, the U.W. seismologists had to draw conclusions about what they could not see. They learned to recognize certain characteristic patterns of seismic activity that precede and accompany eruptions. By examining the seismograph's distinctive patterns of squiggles — called seismograms or "seismic signatures" — they were able to distinguish between deep earthquakes and shallow earthquakes; they

learned to identify the sustained rhythmic vibrations called harmonic tremor, as well as the signatures of the explosions themselves, ice and rock avalanches, and, for that matter, snowmobiles racing past the monitoring sites, helicopters hovering overhead, and the footsteps of curious backpackers checking out the monitoring stations.

They found it was often possible to predict volcanic activity by watching the rate and type of seismic activity. A few days to two weeks before most eruptions, medium- and low-frequency earthquakes occur at shallow depths within the volcano and gradually increase in number and size. Then, just hours before eruptions, the seismic activity accelerates rapidly. By constantly monitoring the movement of the earth, seismologists have been able to give short-term predictions of a number of the eruptions that have followed the big one on May 18. But puzzles still exist. Harmonic tremor, usually regarded as a tip-off that magma is on the move, has accompanied only some of the subsequent eruptions of Mount St. Helens. For some reason, the presence of the new dome, which plugs the volcano's vent, seems to halt the harmonic tremor.

Swanson has continued to concentrate on deformation—the tendency of a volcano to move, crack, and tilt as the magma rises beneath it. During the eruptions after 1980, Swanson discovered that the rising magma inflated the lava dome and shoved the crater floor against the walls, producing cracks and uplifted blocks, or thrusts.

He went inside the crater six weeks after the eruption to set up targets for measuring devices. When he jumped out of the helicopter, the ground was so soft he sunk up to his knees in ash, so hot he couldn't stand still. He had to march in place while he worked to keep his feet from burning. Armed at times with instruments no more technical than a steel measuring tape, Swanson measured deformation on the floor of the crater day after day, theorizing that the rate of changes in the cracks and crevices in the floor would correlate to eruptive activity. They did. Following each of the eruptions after the May 18 blast, new cracks appeared on the crater floor, radiating out from the new dome like spokes from the hub of a wheel. Swanson measured the width of the cracks and found that they grew continually wider between eruptions and then, starting two to three weeks before an eruption, spread rapidly. The rate of deformation made it possible to tell when eruptions were coming. Until rockfalls made the cracks impossible to see, the accelerated spreading was used to predict several eruptions from 1981 to 1983, from three to nineteen days in advance.

The lava dome as it appeared in July 1980, heated to red-hot incandescence. This incarnation of the dome was destroyed in a subsequent eruption. *Inset:* USGS team members on top of the lava dome in 1985, taking measurements to predict future activity.

Since then, geologists have been able to use the dome in a similar manner and continue the prediction program based on deformation results. "The big difference," Swanson says, "is that we had to forsake the steel tape measure for an electronic one—the so-called Electronic Distance Meter, or EDM." By measuring distances from points on the crater floor to points on the dome, geologists are able to tell how much the dome is moving. This has proved to be a highly successful technique, one that is really no different than that used with the cracks and thrusts, except for the tools involved.

Deformation also is noted with sensitive tiltmeters, used to measure changes in the slope of the crater floor. Tiltmeters have been installed all around the crater and constantly radio information back to the USGS in Vancouver. Tilting of the crater floor began several weeks before each eruption in 1981 and 1982, accelerated a few days before and, on several occasions, abruptly reversed direction shortly before the eruption began. Tiltmeters are especially valuable because they monitor the volcano constantly and provide information in the winter when other methods are impractical.

Other researchers are trying to piece together clues from the emission of gases such as sulfur dioxide, hydrogen, and carbon dioxide. When the sulphur dioxide content of the gases goes up, it seems to indicate that magma is making its way to the surface. It is not always clear, however, whether the gases come from the magma or shallow hot spots in the dome.

According to Swanson, some of the biggest advances made in the science of monitoring volcanoes did not involve sophisticated technology, but technique. Working close to the vent is critical, as is getting information quickly—even if the methods appear crude. The steel measuring tape turned out to be one of the geologists' most valuable tools. "The lesson we learned over and over again was that you have to do what you can, as fast as you can," Swanson said.

In the days before the May 18 eruption, Swanson and his colleagues were well aware of deformation on the mountain itself—the bulge provided ample evidence of that. But the thought occurred to them that the entire region around the volcano might be bulging or tipping as well. To find out if it was, they nailed yardsticks to stumps and docks along the waterline of Spirit Lake, reasoning that if the earth moved, the lake would tip. "We turned the lake into the world's largest carpenter's level," Swanson said. "We found

Water erosion created dramatic changes in the volcanic landscape after the 1980 eruption, including this 600-foot-deep canyon in the headwaters of the Toutle River.

out that there was no deformation going on, but the point was we had created an instrument that was capable of giving us readings accurate to one part in a million with the most basic tool you could imagine. We didn't even have to buy the yardsticks. When the guy at the store heard what we wanted to do with them, he gave them to us."

Even with the advances that have been made, there are significant shortcomings in the art of second-guessing volcanoes. It's still impossible to predict how explosive an eruption will be, and so far, no one has figured out a way to tell how long the eruption will last once it starts.

"We've learned to recognize certain patterns that precede eruptions," USGS scientist Steven Brantley said in 1989. "We can see them coming. But what triggers a certain batch of magma to move? We still don't know."

Backward glances are inevitable. If scientists had known in 1980 what they know now about the patterns that precede eruptions on Mount St. Helens, could they have predicted what happened that day?

Steve Malone says he doesn't think so. "We've gone back through the records again and again, and there was nothing there. We still see nothing for the 18th. The avalanche short-circuited the normal seismic buildup. Given the same situation in repeat, we couldn't do anything very much different."

Swanson is less circumspect. "No," he says without hesitation. "That still would have taken us by surprise."

Thomomys talpoides, otherwise known as the Northern pocket gopher, survived the eruption of Mount St. Helens underground, and by mixing ash with underlying soil, played a critical role in bringing the devastated area back to life.

BACK TO LIFE

Disasters have a way of producing heroes, sometimes out of the unlikeliest characters. Mount St. Helens produced a number of heroes, but none nobler than the lowly pocket gopher, a furry, short-tailed rodent about the size of a hamster. With its close-set eyes and weak chin, the gopher was not a typical candidate for heroism; gophers are more often associated with the harm they do to the environment than the good. But the role the gopher played in bringing the devastated Mount St. Helens area back to life transcended both its appearance and reputation.

Before the eruption, colonies of pocket gophers lived in meadows, forest clearings, and lake basins throughout the Mount St. Helens backcountry. They burrowed deep, complicated mazes of tunnels, and lived by snipping off the tender roots of plants. For the short term, they stored wads of nourishment in their expandable cheeks; for the long term they stashed provisions in hidden caches underground.

On May 18, 1980, the day of Mount St. Helens's cataclysmic eruption, the ground in the high Cascades was still covered with patches of snow. The pocket gophers were snug in their burrows. When the mountain erupted, most plants and animals above ground were killed—shriveled by waves of heat hot enough to crack rocks and blown away by hurricane-force winds.

Most of the pocket gophers died, too—either roasted or suffocated in their burrows. But in some isolated spots, places where the topography and the cover of snow protected them from the full effect of the blast, a few pocket gophers survived. Afterward, they scuttled, blinking, up into the destruction, like survivors of a nuclear explosion.

The devastation the gophers saw around them—no doubt dimly with their tiny, nearsighted eyes—was an environmental catastrophe of overwhelming proportion. Cool, green forests had been transformed into a putty-grey desert. Lakes had become brackish sinks that smelled like rotten eggs; rivers and streams were buried in hot mud. Blowing, gritty ash filled the air. Trunks of the largest trees were strewn over the ground, half buried in ash; all other plants—mosses, ferns, shrubs, and wildflowers—had simply disappeared.

The Washington State Department of Game estimated that 1,500 elk, 5,000 black-tailed deer, 200 black bears, 11,000 hares, 15 mountain lions, 300 bobcats, 27,000 grouse, and 1,400 coyotes were killed that Sunday morning. Miles from the crater, heavy ashfall caused the deaths of many more. The heat and the ash wiped out incalculable numbers of birds and insects, damaged 26 lakes, and killed some 11 million fish.

The pocket gopher, bane of tree-planters and bad boy of suburban lawns, was an improbable hero in this setting. But the gophers rose to the occasion. Using their burrows as fallout shelters, they lived through the summer of 1980, eating the roots and bulbs of plants whose tops had been blasted away. They burrowed through the new ash like little plows, mixing it with the organically rich, underlying soil, and bringing up spores of fungi that make it easier for plants to absorb nutrients. Wherever the gophers went they left fertilized and cultivated plots where wind-borne seeds could drift in and take root.

Plant seeds landed on the pocket gopher mounds and transformed them into oases of fireweed, lupine, and thimbleberry. The plants attracted insects, which attracted birds. Foraging mammals ventured in from the periphery to explore and hunt. And the cycle of life began anew.

The pocket gophers didn't single-handedly restore the blast zone. But the process they initiated in the recovery of Mount St. Helens is perhaps the best example of the sorts of chance encounters and unpredictable sequences that are slowly bringing the land around the volcano back into balance. The gophers epitomize the complex symbiotic relationships between survivors of the eruption and colonizers—those species that moved into the devastated area after the explosion. Together, survivors and colonizers worked to heal the damaged environment more quickly than anyone thought possible.

Three years after the eruption, 90 percent (230) of the plant species and nearly all the mammals believed to have inhabited the area before 1980 had been observed in the devastated area—even though they existed in much fewer numbers and wildly different orders of dominance. A decade after the eruption, bits of green were scattered throughout the blast zone. The little oases still seemed tentative and frail when viewed in the overall context of the destruction, but nature was clearly on its way to recreating what had been destroyed on May 18.

The process of rebirth was watched with fascination by hundreds of biologists, entomologists, mammalogists, zoologists, mycologists, and ecologists who flocked to the volcano after the eruption. For them, the devastated land around Mount St. Helens represented the chance of a lifetime.

"It's a natural experiment," said forest ecologist Peter Frenzen, "an experiment too expensive and impractical to produce. Imagine the grant request: 'What I want to do is take every bit of vegetation and animal life off 100,000 acres of forest and subalpine meadows. And then I want to come in and cover it with new material so we can monitor returning life.' They'd say, 'Well, it's an interesting idea, but obviously impractical.' Here, it's been done for us."

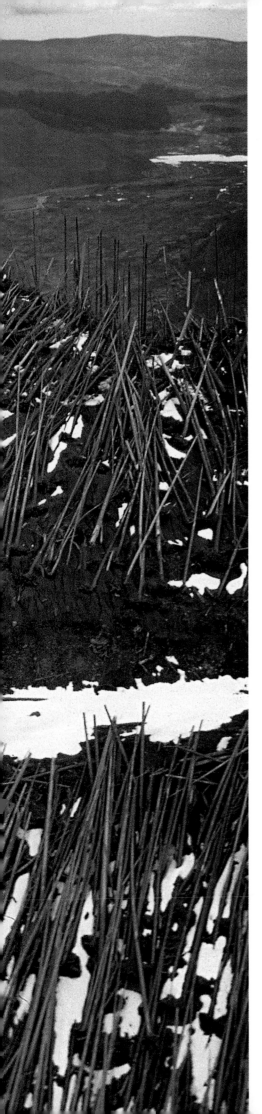

Frenzen works for the U.S. Forest Service, the federal agency that manages the Mount St. Helens National Volcanic Monument. Congress passed legislation creating the 109,900-acre monument in August 1982, after a bitter struggle between environmentalists and timber interests over how much land should be included. The purpose of the monument designation was to protect the volcano and other distinctive volcanic features for public use and scientific research.

Frenzen's official title is "Monument Scientist," meaning it is up to him to coordinate all of the scientific research within the monument boundaries. He is responsible for keeping track of several hundred experiments being conducted by scientists from around the United States. Frenzen works out of the monument headquarters, a collection of prefabricated office buildings and trailers pulled together near the tiny town of Amboy on the south side of the mountain.

Frenzen is a straightforward but careful man, with the slightly distracted air of someone who has just remembered he should be doing something else. Part of his job as monument scientist is grappling with the Big Picture—attempting to put the individual studies on the mountain into some sort of larger perspective that encompasses the nature of life on earth. In his Amboy office, surrounded by computer printouts, animal traps, field notebooks, and a blizzard of paper, Frenzen rarely has time for that. When he's not in the blast zone, doing his own research, Frenzen's hands are kept full organizing the activity on the mountain so geologists don't trample through biologists' test plots and vice versa.

Several hundred different research projects have been set up on or near the volcano since the 1980 eruption. The blast zone bristles with stakes marking research plots; bright red and yellow plastic flags flutter in the breeze; hunks of steel pipe, antennas, and odd sculptural contraptions poke out of the pumice, accentuating an already otherworldly atmosphere. The topics for study traverse the width and breadth of the life sciences, ranging from analyses of the reproductive habits of rough-skinned newts to the origin of life on the planet. What are the effects of suspended and deposited volcanic ash on survival and behavior of stream insects? How have the population dynamics of Roosevelt elk been altered in the blast zone? What are the capacities of plants to move upward through volcanic ash? What is the process by which pumice is transformed to soil?

Ecologists, who take the broad view, asked a question that encompassed many of the others: How does a complex environment go about recovering from profound disturbance? The destruction left by the volcano was in a

sense a wound on the surface of the earth, an abrasion on its highly evolved epidermal layers. Monitoring the slow march of healthy organisms back toward the center of the crater, ecologists believed, could add any number of conceptual pieces to the complex puzzle of life.

By observing the natural succession of plants and animals, by examining their interrelationships as they began reestablishing themselves in the inhospitable terrain, the scientists hoped to gain insights applicable to other environmental catastrophes—man-made disturbances like strip mines, oil spills, and clearcuts; and natural disasters like wildfires and windstorms. Understanding the natural healing process, they reasoned, would better equip them to nudge things along when necessary.

In the abstract, seeking knowledge in the blast zone was an intriguing, even romantic, quest. Actually gathering the data, however, was anything but.

Access to the blast zone was tightly restricted after the eruption because no one could say with any confidence what the mountain would do next. During the summers of 1980 and 1981, the volcano erupted or extruded lava seven different times, making research an exciting activity in more ways than one. Access was by helicopter only, and regulations required that researchers stray no farther from the aircraft than they could run in 15 minutes. To simplify logistics, scientists sometimes were ferried into the blast zone in groups of 40 to 60 at a time.

Because they travel so efficiently on the wind, insects, such as the short-horned grasshopper (*above*) and the ladybug (*right*), are among the most numerous immigrants into the blast zone. Studies by entomologists indicate that as much as a half ton of insects land on the blast zone each summer. Few survive for long, but they provide food for other organisms and contribute significant amounts of carbon and nitrogen to the developing soil.

The volcano was a miserable place to work. There was no shelter from the sun and wind, and no water. Getting from place to place meant crawling over or under tree trunks that had been strewn like pick-up sticks, or hiking, like Lawrence of Arabia, across miles of desertlike terrain. The fine ash, a certain portion of which always tended to be airborne, filled the researchers' ears and eyes with grit and crunched between their molars at lunchtime. Being a scientist in the blast zone meant long days doing tedious, repetitive chores in one of the harshest environments imaginable. Frenzen spent a good part of the first three years after the blast on his hands and knees in the ash, counting conifer seedlings in 225-square-meter plots.

But the physical discomfort was not the worst of it. Being in the blast zone took a psychic toll as well. The overwhelming feeling was the ever-present proximity of death. Death was everywhere and stretched to every horizon. Working next to the volcano was in many respects like working in a cemetery.

Yet, bad as the blast zone was, it was not the total graveyard most biologists had expected. The first researchers went into the blast zone expecting no survivors. They expected, as Frenzen put it, to see life start back from zero, as if from the beginning of time. They assumed that the recovery would proceed as organisms from the outside—pioneers from the surrounding forests—gradually made their way back in.

What they found instead was that a surprising number of organisms had survived the blast. The pocket gophers were not alone.

Two and one-half weeks after the eruption, Jerry Franklin, chief plant ecologist at the Forest Service's Pacific Northwest Forest and Range Experiment Station in Corvallis, Oregon, along with two other top Forest Service scientists, research geologist Frederick Swanson and ecologist James Sedell, climbed aboard a Huey helicopter and made the first scientific foray into the blast zone. "We were all a little nervous, but excited, too," Franklin recalled. "We didn't know what to expect. Our first stop was Ryan Lake [12 miles northeast of the crater]. We got out of the helicopter and stepped across a ditch on the edge of the road and right away we saw fireweed sprouts coming up through the ash. I looked a little farther and saw ants working, then signs of gophers digging and coyote tracks. After that we went over to the Clearwater [Valley] and there, right in the middle of all this unbelievable destruction, with grey, shattered trunks and branches everywhere and the air filled with smoke from smoldering logs, there was a trillium growing. I couldn't believe it. Every time we turned around we saw another

way something had lived through the eruption. I said, 'Oh, my God, this place is covered with survivors.' "

In certain sheltered places not far from the crater, whole communities of plants and animals had survived, protected by the topography and the cover of ice or snow. Utah State University biologist James MacMahon, one of the most articulate and influential of the researchers, discovered one such island of life a few hundred feet above Spirit Lake, in the heart of the most badly battered land.

In the blowdown and scorch zones, even more had survived. Fireweed, thistle, pearly everlasting, and blackberry vines shot up through as much as twelve inches of ash just weeks after the eruption. In a few places, young trees that had been bent over and buried in snow escaped unharmed. Pocket gophers had survived, as had at least 13 other species of small mammals— deer mice, wandering shrews, voles, weasels. On the leeward side of rocks and ridges, and in hollows behind the upturned roots of fallen trees, plant parts still were living below the surface. Ants survived in their underground nests, just as the gophers had. Beetles rode out the storm deep inside 500-year-old trees.

"The message is clear," University of Washington botanist Roger del Moral reported in *Natural History* magazine in 1981. "While it took a beating, life was never obliterated from Mount St. Helens."

For scientists trying to discover and document some sort of model of succession—that is, an orderly procession in which plants and animals would return to reclaim the land—it quickly became clear that the marching order would be extremely complicated. There was no tabula rasa, no even starting point. The closer the researchers looked, the more each square meter of the devastated zone appeared to differ from the others. Instead of a blank slate, what they had was a mosaic of habitats—widely varying little worlds, which no single model of succession would fit.

The single most important revelation, though, was one that flew in the face of textbook knowledge about how recovery would proceed. The recovery would not depend entirely upon the rate at which colonizing species from outside the blast zone made their way in, but would rely to a large extent on the species that had never left—those that had lived through the eruption—and on the physical processes of the earth itself.

Some of the scientists' original exuberance and wonder expressed at the resilience of survivors faded after the first season or two. For some of the plants and animals still alive on May 19, it was less a matter of surviving

A number of organisms survived the volcanic blast because they were underground or covered by snow. Pacific tree frogs, hibernating in mud at the bottoms of lakes, escaped unharmed and repopulated the area afterward. Others, like the woolly bear caterpillar (*above*) and a fireweed plant found growing on the inhospitable pumice plain (*left*), were transported into the blast zone by the wind.

than simply taking longer to die. The pocket gophers, for example, lived out the first two years fairly well, but died off rapidly in the third. Their supply of roots had run out and the weedy plants that reestablished themselves did not contain enough nutrients to support them. Lack of adequate food and shelter took a heavy toll on many other plants and animals.

Other survivors, freed from predators and competition, exploded into weird, unbalanced communities for a time and then either leveled off at a much reduced number or disappeared entirely. A geophysicist doing research near the volcano a year after the eruption recalls hiking over the top of a ridge and seeing an entire hillside move. Looking closer, he realized the movement was not the earth but thousands of toads, squatting flipper to flipper on the ash. They had survived in an embryonic state, under the cover of ice in a nearby lake. There were so many of them that when they hopped, the landscape fibrillated. Other lakes spawned other unusual dynasties. In some, there were legions of rough-skinned newts, in others, hordes of Pacific tree frogs or brown salamanders.

While survivors directed the recovery of Mount St. Helens, colonists played a critical supporting role. Potential colonizers began appearing in the blast zone even before the dust of the eruption had settled. National Guard rescue crews searching for human survivors during the week after the eruption found that wasps and flies had preceded them into the blast zone. Helicopter pilots who landed inside the crater later in the summer reported that hummingbirds dive-bombed them, mistaking their day-glow orange jumpsuits for something sweet and nutritious. Curious deer and elk trotted into the blast zone just days after the eruption, and at the mouths of humid steam vents, heated by the underlying pyroclastic flow, gardens of windblown mosses and ferns took shape with such comparative lushness that botanists began referring to the area as "Fumarole Gardens."

The air was filled with a constant rain of insects, spiders, spores, seeds, and eggs that came drifting in from surrounding forests. Entomologists identified 75 species of spiders on the pumice plain, directly in front of the crater, all of which had come from miles away, hang-gliding on long filaments of web.

But surviving in the blast zone was not easy for pioneering species, as Charlie Crisafulli, resident ecologist at the Mount St. Helens National Monument, pointed out. "It takes a combination of highly specialized characteristics that few species have," he said. To be successful, colonizers not only have to have good dispersive abilities—that is, be able to travel long distances—but they must be able to endure serious hardships once they arrive. "Some [plants and animals] have good dispersive qualities but can't survive when they get here," Crisafulli said. "Other species would do beautifully in this environment but have no way to get here."

Like Frenzen, Crisafulli is an employee of the Forest Service—but he doesn't look the part. Tall and thin, with a full beard and long black braid that hangs down his back, he looks more like a freedom fighter than a forest ranger. Yet Crisafulli is an undisputed authority on all that lives in the blast zone; he is obsessed with the volcano. Two months after the 1980 eruption, he began doing biological research on the pumice plain, directly in front of the crater, and by his own reckoning, he has spent more days there than any other scientist. He can identify more than 300 species of birds, many by song alone. Like some sort of primitive tribesman, he knows where to find water and shelter. "A lot of these other people," he says of his coworkers, "look at the fact they've got a volcano on their district either as a kind of a nuisance or just an okay thing. For me, it's the only reason I'm here."

Crisafulli came to Mount St. Helens as Jim MacMahon's research assistant. MacMahon, Crisafulli's mentor as well as supervisor, took an immediate interest in the pocket gophers and their symbiotic relationship with colonizing plants. He wanted to find out if they were really helping the vegetation and, if so, how much. Consequently, much of Crisafulli's time the first two seasons was spent trapping pocket gophers. He'd set traps out at night, 50 or so at a time. In the morning he'd open them one by one, give each gopher a quick physical, put an identification band on its front paw, and let it go.

Crisafulli's other major research project after the eruption entailed documenting not survivors of the blast but colonists. The only place it was virtually assured that there had been no survivors was on the pumice plain. There, every living thing had been buried in 300 feet of avalanche debris, covered with steaming mud, and finally topped with a superheated flow of frothy rock from deep within the earth. Knowing that any plant or animal found there would have to be a newcomer, Crisafulli and MacMahon hiked across the pumice plain and hovered over it in chartered helicopters after the blast, searching for pioneers that, through whatever bizarre twist or miscalculation, might have landed and taken hold.

After several days of looking, MacMahon and Crisafulli finally found a single lupine plant, alone on hundreds of acres of pumice and hissing fumaroles. Surrounded by devastation and overwhelmed by the specter of the steaming crater looming above it, the lupine looked so green it was almost luminescent. The two scientists regarded it as a minor miracle. Crisafulli carefully measured out a 225-square-meter plot around the plant and pounded hunks of white plastic pipe at each corner. Then he stretched twine around the plot to keep other researchers from inadvertently stepping on the plant.

What enabled the lupine to establish itself and survive, Crisafulli explains, is the species' ability to extract nitrogen from the atmosphere. Because the pumice contained almost no nitrogen, that capacity was indispensable. The first summer the lupine surrounded itself with vigorous shoots, and by winter the plant had grown into a delicate circle two feet across. By the second season the lupine had added enough organic material and nutrients to the soil for it to support other weedy plants—false dandelion, fireweed, pearly everlasting. The foliage acted as a snare for airborne seeds and insects. Yarrow, thistle, and sedges moved onto the plot. Grasshoppers, spiders, and ladybugs crawled around under the leaves.

Watching the lupine became Crisafulli's passion. Over the next 10 years he paid more attention to it than any of the rest of his research projects. He found himself spending his spare time there, often becoming so engrossed that he forgot about the active volcano exhaling vapors above him.

Crisafulli spent hundreds of hours crawling through the plot each summer, counting plants and taking detailed notes on each one's life history. He made a special plywood platform to lie on so he could work without squashing his subjects. To locate each plant accurately, he strung wires back and forth across the plot to make a grid and then assigned each one coordinates, like positions on a bingo card.

By the end of the third growing season, the lupine had formed a solid mat of vegetation in which Crisafulli counted 24,000 individual plants. By the tenth season, the summer of 1989, he had counted a total of 164,000 plants, which burst into vibrant purple bloom and spilled out of the research plot on all sides. In the summer, the plot hummed with bees, heavy with pollen.

Crisafulli stresses that the success of his lupine plant was highly unusual among colonizing organisms. Many other plants and animals, having found themselves in inhospitable terrain, starved to death or failed to reproduce, just as many of the survivors had. But even though many colonizers were unable to establish permanent colonies in the blast zone, their continued appearance there aided the overall recovery. Many insects and spiders, for

The resilience of plant life amazed researchers. Salmonberries (*above*) thrived after pushing upward through 8 to 12 inches of ash, and conifer seedlings successfully established themselves on the nearly sterile pumice plain (*right*) with no apparent source of nitrogen and several miles away from parent trees.

example, found inadequate food and shelter in the blast zone, but offered a steady food supply for others and contributed significant amounts of carbon and nitrogen to the developing soil.

Curious about just how many insects were landing in various parts of the blast zone, a team of entomologists from the U.W. Department of Zoology set out to collect and weigh representative samples. The researchers, headed by research professor John Edwards, used two trapping techniques. In the first they filled shallow trays with golf balls to simulate pumice (real pumice was too dusty and hid tiny insects) and inset them into the pumice plain. In other places, they sank plastic cups into the ash and filled them with ethylene glycol-based antifreeze. The highly toxic antifreeze killed and preserved any insect that happened to crawl, fly, or hop into the cup. The plan was to collect the insects every two weeks, identify them, and weigh them.

The results were skewed at first because thirsty elk and other mammals kept drinking the antifreeze. Edwards tried electric fences around the cups, but the pumice was too dry to ground batteries. The researchers eventually ended up surrounding their traps with barbed wire and, after a great deal of collecting and weighing, arrived at the conclusion that from six to ten milligrams of insects fall per square meter of the monument each day in the summertime. Most were flies, mosquitoes, and gnats. Extrapolating their findings over the entire blast zone, they calculated that approximately one-half ton of insects lands in the blast zone each summer. (No follow-up studies were undertaken to determine the effect of the toxic antifreeze on the elk.)

"The colonizing animals that do best are opportunists and generalists," Crisafulli said. "They can switch hit—they can eat seeds, insects, or green vegetation. They're prolific breeders and not tightly tied to any one habitat." Elk, for example, are highly mobile and move freely in and out of the devastated area. So many elk are in the blast zone, in fact, that some biologists believe them to be hindering the recovery. Hundreds of them congregate year round on the avalanche debris flow along the North Fork of the Toutle River, where the Soil Conservation Service planted grass to prevent erosion. Hundreds more turn up there each fall, seeking refuge from elk hunters. (Elk hunting is allowed in the monument, but not on the avalanche debris flow.) The elk do some good: their hooves break up the ashy crust on the surface and, by causing erosion, help mix old topsoil with the ash; their excrement makes an effective transportation mechanism for seeds. But the elk browse tender new plants unmercifully. "There's no question about it,"

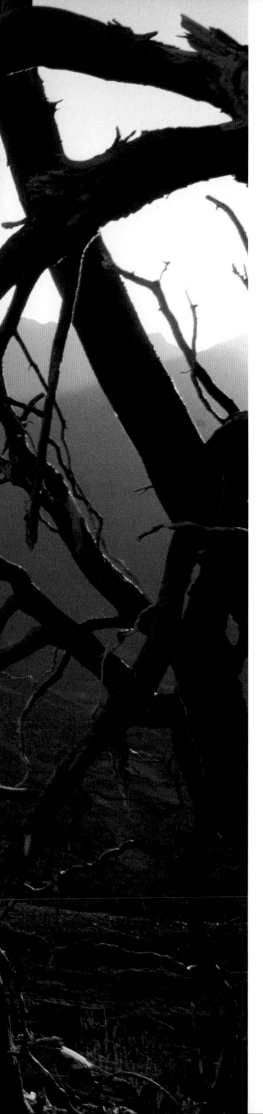

Much of the most useful scientific data from the blast zone comes from constantly monitoring changes over time. *Inset, top:* A forest ecologist measures the trunk diameter of a Douglas fir seedling on the pumice plain and (*inset, bottom*) the length of a white-footed mouse.

Frenzen says, "they're definitely having an impact on the vegetation. They can really tear up the soil."

Birds, the most mobile species of all, are constant visitors. But while there are ample seeds and insects for them to eat, suitable nesting sites are difficult to find. Bird species dependent on old-growth forest for seeds, insects, and nesting sites have not been among the colonizers. They, like other old-growth-dependent species—Douglas squirrels, tree voles, and northern flying squirrels, for example—will not be able to survive in the blast zone until centuries from now, when coniferous trees again become the dominant plant species.

Coniferous trees suffered worst in the blast, and because of their slow growth and the tendency of their seeds to stick close to home—the seeds from conifer cones seldom make it farther than a few hundred yards from the trees that produce them—they have been slow to establish a presence.

Even so, a few Douglas firs and hemlocks, along with hundreds of cottonwoods, maples, and alders, have sunk their roots directly into the pumice crust and the avalanche debris flow, having been transported for miles by the wind, water, and animals. They manage to survive there, even though stunted like bonsais. These trees are in perilous territory: Because of their proximity to the volcano, they are the most likely victims of even minor eruptions, lahars, and pyroclastic flows. When the volcano erupts again, they almost certainly will be swept away. Even in pre-eruption days, coniferous trees had not made the slow climb back up the slopes of the mountain as far as on other Cascade peaks because of Mount St. Helens's frequent eruptions. Before May 18, 1980, the tree line on Mount St. Helens was around 4,200 feet—1,000 feet lower than nearby Mount Adams and 2,000 feet lower than Mount Rainier.

In a helicopter high above the blast zone, Weyerhaeuser forester Dick Ford flits over river drainages and ridges, surveying the signs of recovery below. Ford was in charge of Weyerhaeuser's Mount St. Helens timber operations in 1980 and saw 36,500 acres of his company's trees felled in a matter of minutes. Now, he looks down with satisfaction on his company's replanting efforts outside the boundaries of the national monument. The resilience of nature is phenomenal, Ford says. As an example, he points out that the South Fork of the Toutle River, so scoured and muddied during the eruption that all fish habitat was wiped out, now has as many winter steelhead-spawning areas as any stream in Washington state.

Successfully established plant colonies (*left*) act as snares to trap airborne insects, which in turn attract birds and foraging mammals like the golden-mantled ground squirrel (*above*). Individually thriving patches of vegetation spread fingers of green toward one another and eventually will combine to form a continuous carpet of life.

According to state fisheries biologists, the success of the steelhead in the South Fork is largely due to fishing restrictions that have excluded the sport fishermen who used to stand elbow to elbow along the banks of the Toutle River. But that is not the lesson Ford finds. "The point," he says, "is that nature can take a lot more punishment than we give it credit for. Animals have a remarkable ability to adapt to changes in the environment."

The tenacity of the plants and animals returning to Mount St. Helens certainly has been a factor in the recovery, but according to the scientists who have done most of the research there, viewing the process in terms of the ability of organisms to adapt to change misses the point in an important way. The critical element in survival has been variety—variety in the range of destruction and variety in the forms of life subjected to it.

Mount St. Helens is recovering because of intricate relationships among plants, animals, and the earth—elaborate linkages that usually are far more difficult to see. On the volcano it is more obvious how each act affects others: windblown seeds collect in the footprints of elk; melting snow washes away ash and exposes fertile soil; fallen trees stop erosion. "There are relatively few players here," says Frenzen, "so it's easier to see the relationships. The contrasts are starker. It's easier to figure things out."

The knowledge that plants depend on animals to live and vice versa was not attributable to discoveries on Mount St. Helens, although some interactions became clearer. A major revelation associated with the volcano was the importance of the role played by the physical processes of the earth itself—wind, rain, snow, erosion. What emerges when Frenzen has time to think about the Big Picture is a vision of the entire planet as an intricately balanced mechanism, balanced not season by season, rainstorm to rainstorm, but on a geological scale that stretches back millions of years. Geological changes are happening fast on Mount St. Helens, making it possible to see effects that normally unfold over millenia. It is an environment in which a mountain is measurably rising, in which molten rock is being changed to soil before our eyes, and in which mountains are visibly washing to the sea.

Volcanic processes and the processes of life may be linked far more intimately than is commonly thought. Evidence discovered two years after the eruption indicates that the first living organisms on earth may have been created in a volcanic setting. In 1982 Oregon State University microbiologist John Baross discovered microorganisms flourishing under rocks in the 208-degree heat of Mount St. Helens's fumaroles. The bacteria he found

Roosevelt elk (*above*) are among the most successful colonizers of the blast zone because of their great mobility. By breaking up the volcanic crust with their hooves and transporting seeds in their feces, the elk help create thriving pockets of vegetation (*right*) in otherwise barren parts of the blast zone. *Overleaf:* The colorful fireweed, which sprouts from rootlike stems called rhizomes and is an energetic pioneer in areas decimated by forest fires and clear-cut logging, was one of the first plants to brighten the volcanic blast zone. Scientists found fireweed sprouts poking through the ash just days after the eruption.

Against the monotonous grey hues of the volcanic landscape, the flamboyance and variety displayed by individual plants make them stand out as distinct miracles.

there, happily making slime trails in the intense heat, bore a striking resemblance to 3-billion-year-old Precambrian fossils, and to organisms recently discovered at volcanic grottos deep in the ocean.

The similarities led Baross to suggest that submarine hot springs may have been the original Garden of Eden. The intense heat and confluence of chemicals are right, he notes, to have set off a sequence of reactions that began with methane, ammonia, and hydrogen, led to the gradual formation of amino acids, then proteins, complex polymers, organized structures capable of metabolism, and on to living, reproducing beings.

Viewed in that light—as evidence of the powerful renewal of the earth, and quite possibly as the great incubator of all life—the Mount St. Helens blast zone seems a distinctly less alien place.

The Aquatic Environment

As on land, the effects of the eruption on lakes near Mount St. Helens varied widely, depending on their distance from the crater and whether or not their surfaces were covered with ice and snow. Some, like Blue Lake and Merrill Lake, which had been frozen over at the time of the blast and suffered only ashfall, escaped virtually unharmed.

Others, most notably Spirit Lake, the gem of St. Helens, and so picture perfect it had seemed like a caricature of a mountain scene, were altered totally. When the mountain blew apart, the world's largest recorded avalanche thundered through Spirit Lake. The water flew out of the basin in a wave that splashed 800 feet up the adjacent valley wall.

"The Big Slosh" is what Rich Ray, a forest interpreter, calls it. "It was like what would happen if you ran down the hall and leaped into a full bathtub," he says. "The water flew out of the lake and scoured the mountainsides."

When the water came back down, it brought everything that was loose with it—dirt, trees, rocks, animal carcasses—and deposited it all back in the lake, the bottom of which by that time had risen 300 feet. Superheated gases carrying fragmented volcanic rock poured out of the volcano and flew into the lake on the afternoon of the eruption, raising the water temperature to nearly 100 degrees. All of the fish, their food chains, and habitats were destroyed. A forest of uprooted trees and debris floated in a solid mat on top, convincing aerial observers that the lake basin had been filled. "Spirit Lake Gone," a banner headline in *The Oregonian* declared on May 20.

The lake was not gone, but every bit of life in it was. The water in the new Spirit Lake was 22 times as alkaline as it had been, and, thanks to the readily dissolvable ash and rock particles blasted out of the mountain, it contained high concentrations of manganese, iron, phosphate, sulfate, and chloride, which drastically altered the lake's chemistry.

Like many other lakes in the blast zone, Spirit Lake collected vast quantities of organic matter after the blast. The heat of the blast and the pyroclastic flow cooked the organic juices from the soil and plants and sent them oozing down into the lakes. There, in highly concentrated forms, they simmered and bubbled up some highly potent brews. Oxygen-eating bacteria, slimes, molds, and great explosions of fungi burst forth in horrific shades of crimson, green, and yellow.

Coliform counts exploded. Some of the raging bacteria cultures were identified as pathogens: *Klebsiella pneumoniae*, for example, and *legionella*, the agent of Legionnaires' Disease. Quickly, all of the oxygen in the water was used up, and new dynasties of anaerobic microorganisms (those that do not need oxygen) took over.

Lakes farther away from the crater were not damaged as badly. In some of them, salamanders, frogs, crawfish, and nymphs that had been dormant in the bottom sediment at the time of the blast survived with no apparent ill effects. Where the ice had been thickest and the ashfall light, mink, muskrats, newts, and fish survived, too. Mosquitoes and rat-tailed maggots, both of which breathe through air tubes like skin divers, were not bothered by the chemical changes in the water and survived unharmed.

In a matter of five years, the chemistry of all the lakes, Spirit Lake included, had returned to nearly normal levels. Rainfall, snowmelt, and fresh groundwater diluted the high concentrations of organics, and oxygen was continuously added by photosynthesis and the turbulence of wind and waves. But for long after the eruption, the volcanic ash and rock on surrounding hillsides continued to wash into the lakes, keeping levels of harmful soluble metals high and frequently burying bottom-dwelling organisms.

Ten years after the eruption, most of the trees were still floating on the surface of Spirit Lake, shifting from one end of the lake to the other with the changing winds. Sonar readings indicated that some 20,000 of the trees had settled upright on the lake bottom, their roots dragging them down like anchors to form a ghostly underwater forest. The oxygen levels in the lake had returned to normal, however. Frogs and toads that migrated down feeder streams to Spirit Lake had established healthy populations there. The water quality was high enough once again to support salmon and steelhead—although they no longer had any way of getting there.

"The different recovery rates on land and in the water were remarkable," said Monument Ecologist Charlie Crisafulli. "Ten years after eruption, all of the lakes—Spirit Lake included—had essentially returned to a normal state. The terrestrial recovery, on the other hand, had barely begun."

Above: No part of the blast zone was more radically affected than Spirit Lake. Once the gem of Mount St. Helens, the lake was buried in 300 feet of avalanche debris, heated to 100 degrees by a flow of superheated volcanic rock, and so chemically altered that runaway bacteria made it bubble as though boiling. Yet, in just 10 years, Spirit Lake was once again clear and pure (*left*). Even though its surface is still littered with the remains of a decimated forest (*insets*), biologists say the lake is capable of supporting a normal range of aquatic life.

Below: Road-building equipment scattered by mudflows on the North Fork of the Toutle River, and (*inset*) one of eight Toutle River bridges washed out by floods that followed the May 18 eruption.

MAN AND THE MOUNTAIN

When Mount St. Helens erupted, people around the world heard about Washington state's exploding mountain. What almost no one heard about was a related phenomenon that developed in the volcano's aftermath: exploding mice.

The events leading up to the mouse deaths began about a week after the May 18 eruption. By then it had become clear that the volcano had left an enormous erosion problem at its base. Although a great deal of volcanic material had been blasted into the air, and a great deal more had surged down surrounding river valleys as mud, the ashfall and the mudflows together amounted to less than one-tenth of one percent of the volcanic debris still piled next to the mountain.

That accumulation of debris, 14 miles long and as deep as 600 feet in some places, was what remained of the top of Mount St. Helens after it had plunged to the valley floor. Composed of boulders, bits of old lava flows, sand, gravel, hunks of glacial ice, and tree trunks—all mixed together and heaped in the headwaters of the Toutle River—it constituted what some called "the world's largest sedimentation problem." The North Fork of the Toutle River—hardly more than a creek in the summertime—was carrying sediment downstream at a greater rate than the Nile or the Amazon. Engineers who examined the avalanche deposit estimated the volume of erodible material at approximately 3 billion cubic yards—enough to bury all of downtown Seattle to the height of the Space Needle.

Mild summer rains sent torrents of fresh silt surging down the north and south forks of the Toutle and on into the Cowlitz River, the channels of which were already flattened into muddy chutes by the May 18 mudflows. Unless something were done, winter rains would cause disastrous flooding in Cowlitz County. "If I lived in Kelso or Longview," warned Dick Janda of the U.S. Geological Survey, "I'd keep my ear on the radio all the time."

No public agency in the United States had ever dealt with the sedimentation problems posed by an active volcano before, but there was an agency that had considerable experience with erosion: the Soil Conservation Service. The Conservation Service, formed during the Dust Bowl days of the Great Depression and usually associated with such conservation techniques as contour plowing and crop rotation, proposed to fix the volcanic erosion problem by planting grass on it.

To the horror of environmentalists, the Conservation Service was given $20 million in federal emergency-relief funds to seed and chemically fertilize most of the blast zone and avalanche flow. In July 1980 the Conservation

Service announced the specifics of its plan: It would use helicopters to seed the area with 13 species of grass—including clover, Kentucky bluegrass, birdsfoot trefoil, and creeping red fescue—of which only one (pine lupine) was native to the Pacific Northwest. Scientists, who wanted to see the blast zone recover naturally, were incensed. They howled in protest, and in large part because of their objections, the Conservation Service scaled back its plan from more than 200 square miles to 33 square miles. In September and October of 1980, helicopters swung back and forth over the devastated area, dropping tons of grass seed and fertilizer onto the blast zone and avalanche debris flow.

Most of the seed never sprouted. The powdery fertilizer blew away in great billowy clouds, leaving the seed to fend for itself on the sterile surface. The seed quickly washed off hillsides and ended up in heaps on valley floors. Where grass did take root, it did not stop erosion. Most of the sedimentation was taking place along channels already cut into the debris, and that process was unaffected by grass. Worse, in places where the grass took hold, it short-circuited the natural recovery process by hardening the top layer of the debris, keeping native plants out.

"We ecologists were disgusted," said Jerry Franklin, chief plant ecologist for the Forest Service's Pacific Northwest Research Station. "It was a waste of money, it didn't stop erosion, and it screwed up a nice, clean study of succession."

But, while the seeding was a failure as far as controlling erosion went, it was regarded as a great success by hungry birds and small mammals. The multimillion-dollar erosion project became, in effect, a multimillion-dollar public-assistance program for rodents. Mice, in particular, liked the grass seed. With free food and practically no predators, their numbers increased rapidly.

The Weyerhaeuser Company, which at the time was in the midst of a frenzied effort to replace 45,500 acres of timber destroyed or damaged in the blast, was confronted with legions of mice. In places, tree planters found as many as 100 mice per acre—25 times the normal population. When the grass seed ran out, the mice began munching on the only other available source of food—the bark on Weyerhaeuser's tender young trees.

The timber giant fought back by dropping more seeds—this time oats tainted with a coating of zinc-phosphide. The mice gobbled up the oats. Inside their stomachs, the zinc-phosphide reacted with acidic gastric juices and turned into a gas that required a great deal of room to expand. The mice blew up like balloons and died.

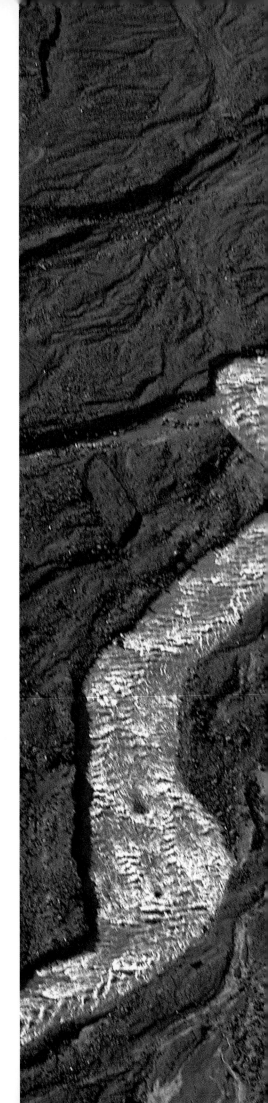

The pneumatic mice illustrate a recurring feature of human attempts to alter the course of nature in the blast zone. In the decade after the eruption, virtually every intrusive action prompted chains of reactions, many of which were utterly unexpected and irrevocable. The moral is similar to one from the tale of Br'er Rabbit and the Tar-Baby: When you're not sure what you're doing, you can get into some very sticky situations with Mother Nature.

While the grass-seeding project was perhaps the most obvious example of human engineering gone awry in the area devastated by Mount St. Helens, it was by no means the only one. During the 10 years following the eruption, public agencies and private corporations spent more than $600 million dollars on efforts to alter the natural course of geological and biological events—projects that included dredging millions of cubic yards of sediment out of rivers, draining lakes, tunneling through mountains, and replacing forests. The engineering efforts ranged in scale from building birdhouses to constructing multimillion-dollar dams.

One of the most urgent problems immediately after the eruption lay at the bottom of the Columbia River. At the point where the Cowlitz River flows into the Columbia, the international shipping channel had been clogged with 50 million cubic yards of mud. The river's depth had been reduced from 40 feet to 14 feet for a distance of two miles. Thirty-one ships were stranded in upstream ports; 50 more were ordered to stand off on their way up the Columbia or to divert their cargoes to other ports. The cost in lost trade to Columbia River port communities grew by hundreds of thousands of dollars each day.

Under the direction of Mike Hay, chief of dredging operations in the Portland District of the U.S. Army Corps of Engineers, three vacuum-style dredging ships were dispatched to the Columbia, where they began working 24 hours a day, sucking up wet mud from the bottom of the river and dumping it downstream. Fully restoring the channel took seven months of digging.

Meanwhile, Hay moved his line of attack to the Cowlitz River, where sediment had reduced the channel's flow capacity from 76,000 cubic feet per second to 13,000 cubic feet per second, and winter floods were almost a certainty. Within weeks, the Corps signed dredging contracts with 28 private companies, assigning each a section of the river to clean out.

The need for immediate labor was so great that some of the companies hired by the Corps had no experience whatsoever with dredging or working

Water in the upper Toutle River valley carves a new channel in the avalanche debris flow.

around rivers. One section of the Cowlitz was dredged by a shopping mall developer, several others by road builders. Dredging equipment was imported from every western state. Machinery normally used for moving timber was retrofitted to move mud.

Within three weeks of the eruption, dredges, draglines, and backhoes lined the banks of the Cowlitz River for 21 miles. With winter rains just four months away, most of the contractors worked two 10-hour shifts a day, six days a week. Upstream in the Toutle, where the flow was lower than the Cowlitz, bulldozers moved short sections of the river 50 to 100 feet out of its normal channel to get it out of the way, dug large pits in the riverbed to trap sediment, and then put the river back again. On the Columbia, Cowlitz, and Toutle rivers combined, dredgers were removing an average of 500,000 cubic yards of sediment a day.

"It was incredible," Hay remembers. "I mean, just the money alone was unheard of. In the Portland district we were used to spending our $20 million a year in basic dredging contracts, and here we had $235 million in one summer."

The problem, of course, was finding places to put the mud once it was out of the rivers. Along the relatively undeveloped Toutle, contractors could dump the spoils just about anywhere they pleased. But along the Cowlitz, which was lined with homes, farms, and businesses, finding suitable disposal sites was difficult.

Various solutions were devised for disposing of the dredged mud. Some of it was pumped through pipelines to destinations nearly two miles away. Wherever the engineers dumped the mud, they ran the risk of destroying wetlands, creating more erosion problems, or complicating natural drainage patterns. Most of the dredge spoils were piled along the banks of the Cowlitz as levees, creating sandy bluffs high above the surrounding countryside. One of the best views of the town of Castle Rock was from the new banks of the Cowlitz River, where it was possible to look down on the roofs of houses below. The heaps of dried mud steadfastly resisted vegetation. Ten years after the eruption, the Cowlitz was lined with an incongruous sandy desert, dotted here and there with sprigs of Scotch broom.

As the digging progressed, the Corps was formulating a plan to stop the sedimentation problem at its source. The volcano and the avalanche debris clearly had the ability to fill the rivers faster than the Corps could dig them out. To hold back the mountain of sediment below Mount St. Helens, the Corps decided to build a wall in front of it—a debris dam meant to slow the

The eruption filled the lower Cowlitz and Columbia rivers with mud, running international freighters aground in the Columbia (*above*) and creating a sedimentation problem in the Cowlitz that required 10 years of dredging to resolve (*left*). *Below:* Unsure of how much erosion to expect from the volcano, researchers invented a new device to monitor ash movement and installed hundreds of them in creeks and gullies.

runoff from the avalanche long enough for the sediment to drop out. The Army engineers chose a site just beyond the toe of the avalanche deposit and, by dynamiting a nearby rock knoll, produced enough material to build a 43-foot wall from one side of the valley to the other—a distance of well over a mile. In the smaller South Fork of the Toutle River, where the sedimentation problems were less extreme, the engineers built a smaller debris dam—600 feet long. Together, the two dams cost $21 million. But they didn't work.

The first heavy rain of the 1980 winter season, on Christmas Day, brought down a torrent of gravel, shattered tree trunks, and mud from the mountain. The flood burst through the new debris dams, hardly pausing, and carried 9.5 million yards of new sediment down the Toutle River.

On the South Fork, the dam was repaired and maintained until September 1981. In 1982 it was removed to allow fish upstream to spawn. On the North Fork, the Corps responded by building a bigger dam—four times higher and three times more expensive. The new $60 million debris dam, officially referred to as the Sediment Retention Structure, is located downstream from the ruins of the old dam at a point just short of the North Fork's confluence with the Green River, 17 miles from the crater. There, the Corps blasted the cliffs on either side of the North Fork to bare rock and built a barrier of earth and concrete 125 feet high between them. The surrounding cliffs were sprayed with a material called "shotcrete"—concrete sprayed

from high-pressure hoses—a substance often used to create artificial bear dens in zoos. Designers of the Sediment Retention Structure, which was completed in November 1989, say the dam will handle mudflows at least as large as the one initiated by the May 18 eruption and floods bigger than any the North Fork ever has produced.

On the spillway of the new dam, Scott Apple steers a white Suburban wagon bearing an Army Corps of Engineers insignia in a wide circle, its wheels describing the approximate swing to the right that hydrologists say a mudflow would take if it were to hit the dam. Apple, the Corps chief of construction on the dam project, was in Saudi Arabia working on another project during the eruption of Mount St. Helens and most of the Corps's post-eruption battles with erosion. His knowledge about what happened in May 1980 is sketchy, but he knows the dam inside and out. Even if a major mudflow never arrives, he explains, the reservoir behind the dam is expected to fill with sediment by 2035. When it's full, it will hold 258 million cubic yards of sand that will reach five miles upstream. Whether the sediments are deposited in one day or gradually until 2035 depends largely on the volcano. When the debris dam is full, Apple says, there will be two options: build the dam taller or dig out the accumulated sediment behind it.

If it were dug out, where would the sediment go?

Apple grins and looks around at the steep rock walls of the valley on either side of the dam. "I don't know where you'd put it," he says. "Two hundred and fifty-eight million cubic yards is a lot of dump trucks." (It is 25.8 million dump trucks, to be exact—enough to circle the globe six times, bumper to bumper.)

Faced with expensive and possibly deadly erosion problems, the Army Corps of Engineers built a mile-long debris dam across the North Fork of the Toutle River (*above*). When the dam failed after the first heavy rain, in December 1980, the Corps reinforced it with additional concrete and earth (*above right*). The dam promptly failed again.

The volcano is not the only threat facing the dam. When the avalanche thundered down the side of Mount St. Helens in 1980 and lodged itself in the Toutle River valley, it blocked a number of feeder creeks that flowed out of surrounding ravines and valleys. Water backed up behind the avalanche material, forming several new lakes (and greatly enlarging Spirit Lake). Most of the new lakes were little more than ponds, but those formed on two of the tributaries—Coldwater Creek and South Castle Creek—held more than 100,000 acre-feet of water. If any of the large lakes were to break through the avalanche material holding them in, mud and water would surge over the dam as if it weren't there.

Realizing this, engineers began to cast a wary eye not only at the erodibility of the avalanche debris, but at its overall structural integrity. Test bores into the material indicated that Mount St. Helens had essentially been turned upside down in the blast. What had been the top surface of the volcano's slopes—organic material, weathered rocks, sandy soil—had slid off first and was now on the bottom of the pile. Burying it were bigger chunks of glacial ice and boulders—some as large as houses—that had been blasted out of the mountain by the explosion. On top of that was a third layer, approximately 70 feet deep, composed of the fine silt and sand that had been suspended in the air and then had drifted down as a topping.

This upper layer was so light and unstable that natural runoff from the mountain cut through it as though it were flour, carving it into cavernous holes, tunnels, arches, and grooves. As the chunks of buried glacial ice melted, deep craters opened up on the surface. "It was weird walking around up there," Hay remembers. "There were gullies 20 feet deep— trenches that were lined with this fine, chalky, tan-colored material. There were sinkholes all over the place from the melting ice. You didn't know what you were walking on."

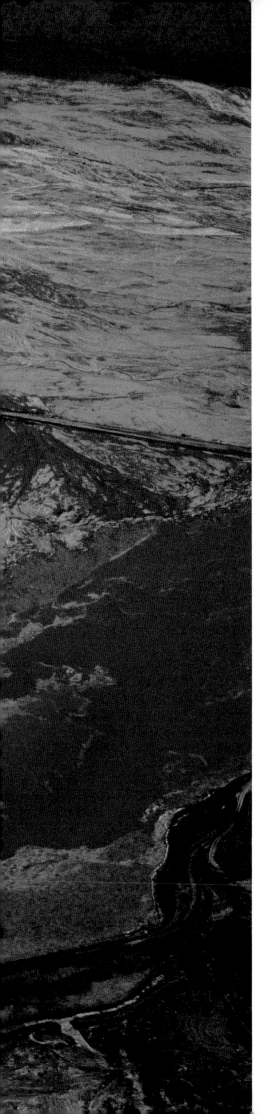

Efforts to stop the flow of volcanic material down the Toutle River cost more than $500 million over 10 years and included massive earth-moving operations at the base of the avalanche debris flow (*left and inset top*). Meanwhile, the Weyerhaeuser Company rebuilt its devastated logging camps (*inset bottom*) and began salvaging 850 million board feet of felled timber.

The better the composition of the debris avalanche was understood, the more precarious the lakes seemed to be. While initial engineering reports warned that the material was holding "like concrete," more detailed analyses warned that it was only a matter of time before the lakes would burst through the rubble and go cascading down the North Fork of the Toutle River. The Corps bulldozed and blasted outlets for most of the new lakes. But that was not possible for Spirit Lake. Adding to the growing sense of urgency was the unexpectedly rapid rise of the water level in Spirit Lake; two years after the eruption the level of the lake had risen 60 feet, doubling the amount of impounded water.

If the dam of rubble holding Spirit Lake were to give way, consulting hydrologists said, the flow of water coming down the tiny valley of the North Fork would surpass 2 million cubic feet per second—more than twice the normal flow of the entire Columbia River and more than any dam could be expected to withstand. Mudflows 10 times greater than those that followed the May 18 eruption would sweep down the valley, drowning the towns of Kelso and Longview in 20 feet of muddy water. The flood would almost certainly take out the Interstate 5 freeway, the Burlington Northern Railroad tracks, and most likely the Port of Longview.

Just three months before the rains of the third winter were to start, Spirit Lake looked like a disaster waiting to happen. Cowlitz County installed $750,000 worth of new flood-warning sirens along the river. President Ronald Reagan officially declared an emergency in August 1982, and with $7 million in federal funds, the Corps arranged to begin pumping water out of the lake.

Pumping Spirit Lake sounded simpler than it turned out to be. Just getting to the lake was a major logistical problem. Every access route had been destroyed in the eruption. Working rapidly, the Forest Service scraped and blasted a precarious road down a cliff in front of the crater. The contractor trucked in mobile homes, 20 heavy-duty diesel pumps, a 150-foot barge, and 600,000 gallons of diesel fuel, and set up a temporary pumping village directly in front of the steaming volcano.

Water from the lake was pumped through 3,450 feet of pipe across the debris flow to the North Fork of the Toutle at a rate of 5,400 gallons a second. Pumping continued for three years, 24 hours a day, burning 3,000 gallons of fuel each day and three million in dollars each year to keep the lake at what engineers considered a safe level.

The pumping effort came with some costs other than dollars. Scraping the road left permanent scars on the ridges fronting the volcano, just a month after Congress had declared 109,900 acres of the blast zone a national monument, directing the Forest Service "to protect the geologic, ecologic, and cultural resources ... allowing geologic forces and ecological succession to continue substantially unimpeded." The outflow from the pumping pipeline destroyed an intensively studied research site on the pyroclastic flow. And, according to ecologists, the work crews who lived in the pumping village on the lake left an unfortunate biological legacy. Because they wanted fresh eggs for breakfast, workers brought live chickens into their compound. To feed the chickens, they brought in grain, which later sprouted, introducing exotic grass species into the blast zone. The grain also attracted a great number of mice. To get rid of the mice, the workers brought in cats. By the time the pumping crew packed up and left, biological researchers studying natural succession in the blast zone had a number of disruptive variables inserted into their data sets.

Involved as it was, the pumping operation was simple compared to the Corps's permanent solution for Spirit Lake. To keep the water level low, the Corps decided to fit Spirit Lake with an artificial drain pipe. The best place for it, they decided, was through Coldwater Ridge—a route that entailed tunneling through 1.6 miles of solid rock. From July 1984 to May 1985, contractors drilled through the ridge with a 12-foot rotating boring machine nicknamed the "mole," which was capable of gnawing through the rock at a rate of 80 feet per day. When the tunneling crews reached Spirit Lake, the water gushed through Coldwater Ridge and then down into the North Fork of the Toutle. The lake was lowered approximately 20 feet to a "safe" level of 3,440 feet above sea level—still 200 feet higher than it was before the May 18, 1980, eruption.

Apple's boss, Mike Hay, regards the new tunnel and debris dam as a solution to the hazards presented by the volcano—at least for the foreseeable future. "It's a fix," he says. "There's no telling what the volcano is going to do way out in the future, but this will take care of it for as long as any of us are around, that's for sure."

Others are not so sure—about either the dam or the tunnel through Coldwater Ridge. In drilling the tunnel, the mole encountered places where instead of rock there was mud. These were annoyances to the contractor—the blades on the mole couldn't cut through the mud, and the sections had to be dug by hand. In one of those spots it took a crew of 10 workers one month

with shovels, deep inside the ridge, to get to solid rock again. According to geologists, the significance of the mud is far greater than a mere annoyance. The mud the diggers encountered marked joints in the mountain — geological faults that run vertically from top to bottom in Coldwater Ridge. They are evidence of the St. Helens Seismic Zone, upon which the ridge and Mount St. Helens itself lie. Movement along the faults would cause the mountain to shift, as it has in the past, and this could block the tunnel. If an earthquake were to coincide with another eruption, Spirit Lake and a good part of the avalanche debris flow would be on their way to the Pacific Ocean, carrying large portions of Cowlitz County with it.

"It might not be the most likely set of circumstances," said USGS geologist Don Swanson, "but it's certainly not outside the realm of possibility."

A more immediate risk, according to geologists, is that one of the biggest lakes formed during the eruption of Mount St. Helens — Castle Lake — will break through its debris dam and gush downstream. The Corps constructed an outlet channel for Castle Lake in 1981, but eight years later, USGS scientists discovered that the avalanche debris damming Castle Lake was heavily saturated with water. An earthquake could cause the debris to take on the properties of liquid and flow downhill, with the lake hard on its heels. The wall of mud would easily overwhelm the new Sediment Retention Structure built by the Corps.

While the Corps's system of dams and tunnels may or may not be enough to keep the volcano and its lakes from coming downriver, it has forced a number of environmental compromises. One of them is that migrating salmon and steelhead, basic elements of the upriver food chain, are no longer able to ascend the North Fork of the Toutle to spawning grounds in upper tributaries. To deal with the problem, the Corps built a Rube-Goldberg fish trap at the bottom of the dam in which salmon and steelhead migrating upstream are shunted into holding pens, lifted in an elevator, and then emptied through a rubber hose into a truck. A driver hauls them around the dam and deposits them upstream.

Theoretically, the young fry and smolts are able to move downstream through the dam, but fish biologists have expressed some doubts. The water

Two years after the eruption, the water in Spirit Lake (*left*) was 220 feet above its pre-eruption level. Fears that the impounded water might break through the dam of rubble holding it in place prompted two massive engineering projects: building a construction camp on the lake to pump out water (*above*) and digging a new outlet through 1.6 miles of rock with a rotary tunneling machine called the "mole" (*inset*).

moves through a concrete chute at such high velocity that the fish may be injured in the process. The Washington State Department of Fisheries has undertaken studies to find out.

While the Corps battled the volcano for control of the rivers, the Forest Service and private timber companies were struggling with an even more complicated problem of biological engineering—replacing the forests destroyed in the eruption. In a matter of minutes the hot winds of the lateral blast had killed virtually every tree on 150,000 acres of timberland north of the volcano—some of which were several centuries old and up to seven feet in diameter.

In all, nearly five billion board feet of timber had been blown down, killed by heat, or otherwise damaged in the blast—an amount roughly equal to the entire annual harvest in the 19 national forests of Washington and Oregon. Even before the eruption column had subsided, Weyerhaeuser foresters were aloft in company helicopters, surveying the damage on their land and plotting ways to begin growing new trees.

The urgency to replace trees was motivated not so much by concern for the ecosystem as it was by economics. The forests that had surrounded Mount St. Helens were among the most productive timber-growing areas in

Before replanting began, private timber companies and the U.S. Forest Service embarked on a massive timber-salvage operation. In September 1980, an army of 1,000 loggers moved into the blast zone. Weyerhaeuser loggers alone removed more than 600 truckloads of salvaged logs a day during the two following summers.

the country. The economy of Southwest Washington had risen and fallen with the timber industry ever since the first white pioneers arrived 150 years before. Of the 150,000 acres of forest land destroyed in the blast, more than half already had been profitably logged and were in various stages of regrowth. The Weyerhaeuser Company, which owned 68,000 acres in the blast zone, already had clear-cut logged all but 12,000 acres of its land, leaving entire square-mile sections of forest shaved. The company had established 26,000 acres of new tree plantations in the blast zone, ranging in age from one to twenty-five years. Weyerhaeuser foresters looked at the damaged timberland as a wasted resource—much as a farmer might view cropland taken out of production. As Weyerhaeuser forester Dick Ford put it, "A forest not growing trees is like having money in your checking account, not your savings account."

Replanting devastated forests was nothing new to timber companies; reforesting their own clearcuts had given them plenty of practice. But the volcano had made the task more difficult in a number of ways. The blast had not only knocked down the trees, it had taken out large sections of the road system that wound like spaghetti through the forest. After the eruption, loggers couldn't get their equipment to the trees. And, while loggers normally strip clearcuts of all vegetation in preparation for replanting, the volcano had not been so tidy. The timber lay in a tangle where it had fallen, making any sort of movement across the slopes, let alone planting trees, nearly impossible.

But the biggest problem was that the volcano had buried the land in as much as two feet of ash and pulverized rock—fragments ranging in size and consistency from talcum powder to popcorn-sized chunks of pumice. Contrary to common belief, the volcanic ash, or tephra, did not contain nutrients that plants could use. The coarser bottom layers of tephra were topped with from 2 to 6 inches of fine, silty material that had drifted down from high-elevation ash clouds. When the top layer got wet, it formed a tough crust that was nearly impenetrable by water.

"We had some doubts about whether it was even going to be possible to grow trees at all," said Gene Sloniker, chief forester for the St. Helens District of the Gifford Pinchot National Forest. "We went out in four-wheel drive vehicles after the eruption and there were so many, many unknowns. I remember my first thought was 'What a catastrophe.' My second thought was 'God, what a challenge—to turn this area back into a productive forest.' We went back and made a search of the literature to see what we could

learn from past experience. There was no literature. We basically found out nobody had ever reforested a volcano before, at least not in this environment."

The first task, at least from an economic point of view, was to remove the trees that had been knocked down and convert them to lumber. Most of the wood was undamaged under the bark, and while the imbedded ash made it hard on chain saws, the wood presented no serious problems at sawmills. Removing the logs was also necessary, according to timber interests, to clear the way for tree-planting crews. While environmentalists and a number of leading scientists argued that many of the downed trees should be left where they were, the timber industry won the dispute with arguments that the dead trees could fuel wildfires and that they were susceptible to infestations of insects—mainly bark beetles—that could infect healthy stands of timber surrounding the blast zone. (Those seemed to be legitimate concerns at the time, but in fact, the ash turned out to be an effective fire retardant, and no outbreaks of bark beetles occurred in areas of the blast zone where logs were not salvaged.)

In September 1980, an army of 1,000 loggers moved into the blast zone and began cutting the felled trees into sawmill lengths and hauling them down the mountain. Over the next two years 850 million board feet of lumber was removed from Weyerhaeuser land alone—most of which was sent to Japan. During peak summer months more than 600 logging trucks a day rolled out of the blast zone, loaded with massive logs. Shattered trunks and those trees that were too small to be used for lumber were crushed with bulldozers and set on fire. The salvage operation ended with the largest slash burns in the history of the Pacific Northwest. At times, more than 1,500 acres were burned at once, filling the southern Cascades with smoke for weeks at a time.

Forest Service officials belatedly acknowledged, in large part because of research on areas of Mount St. Helens left to recover naturally, that fallen timber plays a critical role in the reestablishment of a healthy forest environment. The logs act as natural debris dams, which prevent erosion; in streams, they create quiet pools and nutrients for fish and a multitude of other aquatic organisms. Allowed to decay naturally, the old wood provides

When the broken timber had been hauled away or burned (*above and right*), tree-planting crews began hand-planting new seedlings (*inset, top*). Together, Weyerhaeuser and the Forest Service planted 27.4 million seedlings in the blast zone over a period of eight years. In places, the reflective heat of the sun on light-colored ash was so intense that seedlings had to be protected with sunshades (*inset, bottom*).

food and shelter for birds and insects, and enriches the soil with a time-released supply of nitrogen.

Even before the salvage operation began, silviculturalists at Weyerhaeuser and the Forest Service had established test plots of seedlings of various ages and varieties to see which species, if any, could be grown in the ash and, if so, what special care they required. Weyerhaeuser's first sample plots went in less than a month after the eruption. What Weyerhaeuser and the Forest Service discovered was that if the trees were planted so that their roots could reach mineral soil under the ash, they did surprisingly well. But the planting took some special techniques and a great deal of hand labor.

On National Forest land, much of the planting was done with augers attached to chain-saw motors. The augers, 3 feet long and 4 inches wide, were used to drill holes in the ash and mix it with mineral soil underneath. On Weyerhaeuser land, much of which was flatter, vast acreages actually were plowed with bulldozers that used front-mounted blades to peel away the ash in long parallel rows, 10 feet apart. Tree planters followed along in the furrows with shovels and planted the seedlings one by one. On sunny slopes, the light-colored ash acted like a reflector oven, raising surface temperatures as high as 160 degrees. In those places, workers put a low-grade cedar shingle next to each tree as a sunshade.

Seven years after the eruption, Weyerhaeuser had planted 18.4 million trees on 45,500 acres of damaged timberland, at a cost of $10 million. In slightly more time, the Forest Service had planted 9 million trees on 18,000 acres. Ten years after the eruption, the new trees were 25 feet high in places, making a stark contrast at the borders of the Mount St. Helens National Volcanic Monument, where natural regeneration was proceeding at a far more leisurely pace.

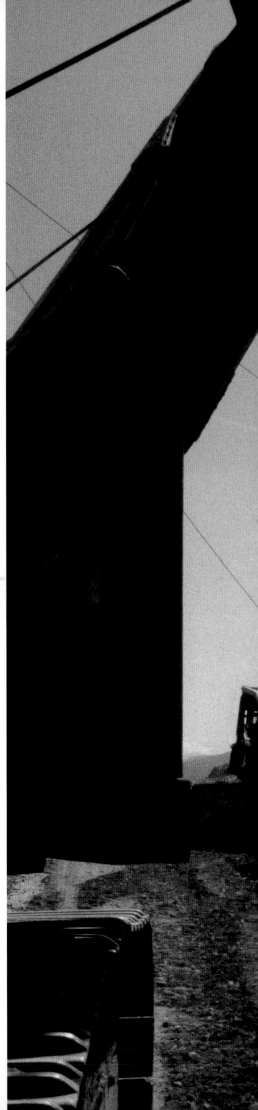

The Weyerhaeuser Company is justifiably proud of its tree farms. Weyerhaeuser, in fact, regularly takes politicians and influential citizens on helicopter tours of their St. Helens plantations, using them as evidence that intensive forest management does not damage the Pacific Northwest forest ecology.

The trees are thriving, but do they really qualify as forests?

Forest Service ecologist Jerry Franklin says no. Franklin was among the first researchers inside the Mount St. Helens blast zone in 1980 and has been responsible for some of the most innovative research there. What he discovered at Mount St. Helens led him to a position highly critical of current forestry techniques.

Franklin concluded that the key to natural recovery in the blast zone was what he called the "biological legacy" — organisms that had survived the eruption. The standard industry practice of clear-cutting and burning is far more destructive to the forest ecosystem than volcanic eruptions, Franklin says, because it leaves fewer survivors. Through research that included inventories of life in the canopies of old-growth forests, standing dead trees, and rotted wood on the forest floor, Franklin and his associates concluded that single-species tree farms are a severely impoverished form of forest, incapable of supporting many species found in more diverse stands. A wide range of species, including spotted owls, pine martens, and 35 to 40 percent of insects and other invertebrates cannot survive in tree farms, yet they are necessary parts of the interrelated whole.

The Forest Service has made some changes since 1980 in the way it approaches logging and reforestation, in large part because of theories substantiated by Mount St. Helens research. The agency's rehabilitation work near the volcano included planting the entire range of naturally occurring tree species rather than just the most marketable ones, leaving patches of standing dead trees where possible, and even going so far as to build raptor perches and birdhouses for species unable to find suitable shelter in young stands of trees.

But in the private sector, changes in planting and harvesting practices met with great resistance. Weyerhaeuser did plant grass and cottonwood trees along streambeds in the Mount St. Helens area to improve wildlife habitat, but has made few concessions to discoveries regarding the importance of maintaining trees of diverse ages in managed forests. "Most people don't realize how much old-growth forest is already protected in Washington state," said Weyerhaeuser's Dick Ford. "There's a whole lot of mis-

understanding out there. We're not up here destroying the forests." Ford says that his company's Mount St. Helens forests will be as intensively managed as the rest of the company's 2.25 million acres in the Pacific Northwest. Techniques will include spraying herbicides, fertilizing heavily, using increasingly intensive genetic engineering of strains of tree seedlings, and maintaining stands of trees that are all the same age.

The point of what has been learned at Mount St. Helens, says ecologist Franklin, is not that humans should adopt a hands-off approach to old-growth forests, but that reforestation should attempt to recreate the entire forest ecosystem, not just commercially valuable timber. Nature's system, while slower, is the best guide to reforestation. "The forest ecosystem is still poorly understood," he says. "When you look back over the last couple of decades and consider all we've learned, you appreciate better what we still don't know—which is most of it."

Geologist Don Swanson has come around to a similar point of view with regard to the Corps's battles with the volcano's lakes and rivers. His love of rocks and a lifetime spent studying the earth's natural forces have made it painful for him to watch the blasting and tunneling and damming taking place around the mountain. In theory, at least, he would have preferred to see nature take its course at Mount St. Helens—to have seen Spirit Lake find its own natural outlet, to see the rivers seek their own courses to the sea, turned by no force other than gravity. "That's the only way you can ensure total safety," he said. "Nature controls itself."

That option, he somewhat reluctantly agrees, was not practical downstream from Mount St. Helens because of the extent of development in the floodplains. Sacrificing the towns of Kelso and Longview, he admits, would have been a bit extreme.

"It's not so much the specifics of this particular case that are important," Swanson said. "It's a whole philosophy—a way of relating to nature. We've gotten trapped in this adversarial relationship with the earth. What mankind has done is to try to best nature. He's sort of challenging nature by doing things like moving onto floodplains.

"We have to realize that we can't control nature. We have to learn to live with it—that way we can learn to enjoy it, or at least appreciate it, and not make value judgments about whether events are 'good' or 'bad.' Ultimately, nature is going to win anyway."

Left: Inside the boundaries of the Mount St. Helens National Volcanic Monument, devastated forests have been left to recover naturally. On a ridgetop near the crater, dead trees are silhouetted by the setting sun 10 years after the eruption. *Below:* Recovery, nature's way. Seeds distributed by the wind slowly colonize the barren pumice plain.

TWENTY YEARS LATER

The visitors' center at Coldwater Ridge is already jammed with people when the three big "Queen of the West" tour buses pull up. Tourists stream from the buses and into the building. They pause momentarily in the lobby to get their bearings and then fan out to the interactive displays.

The visitors' center is dramatically sited directly in front of the dropped jaw of the Mount St. Helens crater, but today the volcano is nowhere to be seen. Thick clouds hide it so completely that the big floor-to-ceiling windows might as well be frosted glass.

But there are plenty of other things to do. There's the theater, with its 16-image screen; there are the banks of video monitors that urge, "Touch the screen to become a colonizer of Mount St. Helens," and a detailed scale model with buttons you can "Push to start the eruption." There's the gift shop, stocked with Mount St. Helens t-shirts and videos and screen-savers, and the cafeteria with its "Truman Burgers" and "Blast Burgers."

And there's a creepy favorite—the robotic ranger, a talking manikin dressed in a U.S. Forest Service uniform. A woman's animated face is projected onto the blank screen of the manikin's head, giving it an eerie, back-from-the-grave effect. On an endlessly repeating tape, she talks about the wonder of life returning to the volcano and warns visitors not to pick flowers or stray off trails.

The recovering plants and wildlife aren't all that is returning to Mount St. Helens. Millions of visitors flock here annually to get a close-up view of the altered mountain. *Top left:* Tourists bustle along the On Winds of Change interpretive walk near the visitors' center at Coldwater Ridge. *Bottom left:* The Johnston Ridge Observatory treats visitors to breathtaking views of the lava dome, crater, and pumice plain. *Above:* The comfortable viewing room in the Coldwater Ridge Visitor Center allows people to relax and try to imagine what the mountain was like before the blast. Every year, visitors from around the world walk through the doors of the center.

"Remember," she says with a lopsided smile, "the monument was established to let nature proceed at its own pace."

This visitors' center, with all of its high-tech displays, is only one of five such centers near the mountain. They are part of a $1.4-billion federal make-over that has transformed Mount St. Helens from disaster to international tourist attraction. The conversion included roads, more than 200 miles of trails, parking lots, a boat launch, and elaborate bridges. More than 13,000 people scramble to the top of Mount St. Helens each year and peer over the crater rim, making it one of the most climbed mountains in the world. In all, three million people a year visit the volcano—a million more than visit Mount Rainier National Park, 50 miles to the north.

The consistent theme in all the visitors' centers is the constantly changing face of the natural world. Their displays show how the volcano transformed the landscape and how plants and animals moved back into the

Left: Four years after the blast, this stunted, ash-covered *Lupinus* struggled to grow on the harsh pumice plain. *Above:* In remarkable contrast to the lonely lupine photographed in 1984, a riot of wildflowers and grasses now carpet the valley below the blast site.

blast zone, gradually bringing the landscape back to life. But that's only part of the story. The recolonization of Mount St. Helens by human beings is an equally remarkable tale. People led the parade of animals that crawled, hopped, and flew back to the volcano. The natural succession of plants and wild animals transformed the volcanic blast zone, yes, but the not-so-natural succession of people has transformed it too—with tourism and traffic.

The fact that three million people visit the mountain each year is enormously gratifying to Van Youngquist, a local dairy farmer who was elected a commissioner of Cowlitz County just weeks before the mountain erupted in 1980. Youngquist has been promoting tourism at the mountain ever since, negotiating deals with federal agencies and currying favor with a long line of congressional representatives, beginning with the legendary power brokers Senators Warren Magnuson and Henry M. ("Scoop") Jackson. He bounced back and forth between Longview and Washington, D.C., carrying

Above left: A dead forest near Ghost Lake. A few Pacific silver fir and mountain hemlock survivors were protected by a hillside of snow on the north slope. *Above right:* No survivors: a portrait of disaster along Forest Road 99 near the blast edge.

a message of prosperity through tourism—an idea he says everybody thought was nuts at first.

"Everybody's first response was, 'Why should we spend good money building anything next to an active volcano?'" Youngquist says. "Nothing would have been built up there if we hadn't pushed it so hard."

Next to a souvenir shop on the Spirit Lake Memorial Highway, the main tourist route that winds up the Toutle River to the volcano, somebody has wrapped one of Johnny Hart's old *B.C.* comic strips in plastic and tacked it to a tree. The strip could have been drawn with Youngquist in mind. In it, one panicked caveman runs up to another, waving his arms and shouting, "The volcano's erupting!"

"Quick!" says the second caveman. "Help me find some boards, a hammer, and some nails!"

"You're going to build us a shelter?" the first one asks.

"No," the second one says, a wild look in his eye, "a souvenir stand."

That's more or less what happened at Mount St. Helens. When Congress declared 109,900 acres around the volcano a national monument in 1982, its intent was to create a multiple-use region. Scientific research, education, and recreation were to share space and resources. In the battle for dominance that took place in the early years of the monument, science put up a spirited fight. Plant biologists and geologists shook their fists at snowmobilers who tore through their research plots. Scientists gamely competed for funding with chambers of commerce and lobbyists for the tourism industry. But it was really no serious contest. In the end, recreation and

Above: Vine maples and huckleberries move into a stand of dead trees near the blast edge in the singe zone. *Left:* Wildflowers hang over a path that winds around the monument. Surrounding snags and downed logs provide a home for many creatures.

education—which, combined by commercial interests, came to mean "tourist attraction"—clobbered science.

The victory can be most clearly seen in terms of money. The National Science Foundation, the primary source of public funds for scientific research, has spent just over $5 million on research projects at Mount St. Helens since 1980. Other public funding for biological research has added about $1 million more. Money for geological research was plentiful in the early years but slowed to a trickle in the 1990s. The grand total of public money spend on scientific research at Mount St. Helens between 1980 and 2000 came to approximately $15 million.

In contrast, the three big, federally funded visitors' centers—at Coldwater Ridge, Silver Lake, and Johnston Ridge—cost $29.1 million. The tourist highway from the Toutle River to Johnston Ridge, a precarious 30-mile route with 10 bridges, cost another $180 million. One single bridge on that road—a half-mile span across Hoffstadt Creek—cost $12.7 million, nearly as much as the entire public contribution for biological and geological research.

Twenty years after the eruption, funding for biological research on the monument is so scarce that scientists cannot even afford to update long-term studies begun immediately after the eruption. Each year, the lone monument scientist, Peter Frenzen, struggles to entice a fresh crop of graduate students and student interns from colleges around the country to undertake research projects on the mountain either for free or in exchange for housing and a minimal stipend.

To be fair, it should be mentioned that, in the interest of scientific research and natural recovery, parts of the monument are closed to tourists. No one is allowed inside the crater without a special permit, for example, and hikers are not supposed to stray off trails anywhere inside the blast zone.

And when the Forest Service built the trails, roads, and visitors' centers,

Left, top to bottom: It's getting better all the time: the slow spread of green across the landscape of Mount St. Helens and Spirit Lake in 1980, 1982, and 1999.
Above: Indian paintbrush and other shrubbery in Norway Pass, with Spirit Lake and the crater of Mount St. Helens in the background.

it took great care to preserve the natural setting. Before contractors built the Johnston Ridge Observatory—the bunkerlike visitors' center at the highest point of the road, near where geologist David Johnston died in 1980—they went so far as to lift up the rocks and blasted trees, store them like precious relics, and, when the construction was finished, lay them back down again. In high-traffic areas, where millions of visitors were expected to finger the real evidence of the volcano's destruction, the Forest Service manufactured durable replicas of trees out of fiberglass. But it's also true that, in 1989, under pressure from sportsmen, the Washington State Department of Wildlife began stocking lakes in the blast zone with rainbow trout, a voracious species not native to high, isolated lakes but favored by sport fishermen. The decision outraged biologists doing research on natural succession in aquatic environments. Finally, a compromise was worked out with the scientific community where accessible recreation lakes were restocked and others were left in natural, unstocked condition.

Van Youngquist retired from public office in 1998. Although he has sold his dairy cows, he still lives on his farm on the bank of the Columbia River, north of Longview. Mount St. Helens is just 35 miles away, and he remembers that it was clearly visible on May 18, 1980. He had just finished his chores that Sunday morning and was walking toward the house. Looking to the east, he saw the dark pillows of the eruption plume rising above the Cascade Range. He barely had time to say to himself "It's gone off" before his wife threw open the door and hustled him inside to the telephone.

The county sheriff was calling. He told Youngquist all hell had broken loose and that he'd better head down to the emergency operations center at the courthouse ASAP.

The next day, Youngquist flew in a National Guard helicopter over the sea of ash and mud left by the blast. It was a surreal trip. The land was so changed that it looked like another country. On the broad gray plain that the day before had been the Toutle River, he spotted a body sprawled in the ash—one of 57 people who died. That made a lasting impression on him.

But what also impressed Youngquist were the hordes of people who could not wait to get close to the volcano to see for themselves what had happened. The urge was so intense and frantic it seemed to him irrational. People were converging on Cowlitz County from all over the world. They drove their cars as close to the devastation as they could and then climbed over barricades and past warning signs to go farther. They set out on foot across mudflows that were still steaming. After the main eruption, a secondary blast tossed a fusillade of 100-pound boulders out of the crater that landed like bombs on the surrounding countryside. The very next day, geologists saw illegal climbers resting in the divots the boulders had made the day before.

When the government opened a legal climbing route to the lip of the crater, climbers swarmed up the mountain in such numbers that they presented dangers to themselves and the natural recovery process. To avoid such stampedes, the Forest Service set up a permit system limiting the number of climbers to 100 a day. People camped out in the parking lot overnight

Just below the Johnston Ridge Observatory, the Toutle River trickles its way through the Hummocks—pointed hills and canyons formed when huge amounts of rock and dirt washed down the mountain and came to rest here.

to be first in line. On at least two occasions, fights broke out between climbing parties when the permits became scarce.

Youngquist never lost sight of that phenomenon. To him, it looked like economic opportunity, a way to pull his county away from its dependence on the waning timber industry. His instincts were correct. Volcano commerce transformed Cowlitz County.

A voice on the public address system at the Coldwater Ridge Visitor Center announces that an interpretive talk by a monument ranger is about to begin in the pavilion, a six-sided glass observation area in the lobby. People cruising from display to display begin coalescing into an audience in front of an earnest young forest interpreter who stands with her back to the big windows. On a clear day, the open side of St. Helens' crater would loom up behind her. But today there is nothing to see but white.

"The volcano is being shy today," she says. "But here's what you would be seeing if it weren't." She lifts a poster-sized photograph of the mountain over her head.

The young ranger could not have been more than a toddler when Mount St. Helens erupted (and, as she says, she was on the other side of the continent when it happened). Her recounting of the eruption—the initial earthquake and avalanche, the sideways blast, the torrents of mud that swept down river valleys, tearing bridges off their footings—is practiced and neat. In her version, Harry Truman, Gary Rosenquist, and David Johnston all are stock characters in what could be a Disney movie: the eccentric but lovable codger, the unemployed taxi driver who struck it rich with his lucky photos, the brave geologist martyred for science.

To illustrate the subterranean workings of the volcano, the ranger uses a bottle of Coca-Cola. As she talks, she shakes the bottle back and forth

The view of Meta Lake from the Norway Pass Trail in 1984 (*left*), and the same view in 1999 (*above*).

until the foam inside is ready to burst. Then, to demonstrate how the mountain surprised geologists by erupting sideways, she points the bottle directly at a woman from New Jersey and pretends she is going to open it. The woman laughs nervously and edges away.

The impression left by the ranger's presentation and by the elaborate displays that surround her is that of an orderly, finely tuned, and predictable model. Call what happened at Mount St. Helens "devastation," and you'll be corrected. This was not devastation, rangers say, but a natural part of the earth's cycle, as inevitable as the falling rain or blowing wind. They prefer to call what happened "a dramatic alteration of the landscape" or "a disturbance."

The monument staff encourages a view that regards the impact area around Mount St. Helens not as a gradually healing wound on the surface of the earth but as something more akin to a change of season. The earth is not seeking some final end point of equilibrium here, but simply passing through changes that recur as predictably as fall, winter, spring, and summer. Disturbance is a way of life for plants and animals living in the Cascade Range, they say.

As Peter Frenzen, the monument scientist, puts it, "Volcanoes do not destroy; they create." By blocking rivers, they create new lakes and wetlands, he says. The ash and pumice they spew out create well-drained, productive soils. Airborne gases contribute to the global carbon cycle.

As the landscape changes, dynasties of species rise and fade upon it, like a cast of characters flitting across a stage. Even at the volcano's most extreme, Frenzen says, when ground temperatures hovered at hundreds of degrees Fahrenheit, microscopic organisms that had been dormant burst into life. To them, the conditions were ideal. "One organism's disaster is another's opportunity," Frenzen says.

It's hard to take issue with that model when one views things from a perspective of geologic time. But on a human scale, the volcanic eruption and its aftermath are much messier—as Frenzen would be the first to admit.

Frenzen, who oversees the research and scientific interpretation on the monument, has adapted gracefully to the transition of St. Helens from scientific laboratory to tourist destination. Aside from some extra weight around the middle, he barely looks older than he did when he arrived on the mountain two decades ago as an eager young graduate student. His hair is still dark and glossy, without a hint of gray. He has successfully channeled a passion for pure science into a passion for education, a role for which he is well suited. He's a much sought after tour guide, equally comfortable on trails or hunched over a microphone in the front seat of a tour bus, providing a running commentary on volcanoes and the ongoing drama of returning life.

Hiking on a trail above Spirit Lake, Frenzen and a group of visitors come upon the remains of two elk, gristle and tufts of hair still stuck to the bones. Frenzen uses the carcasses to illustrate the principle of natural balance. Elk are one of the dozens of species that temporarily found ideal conditions on the changing terrain, only to suffer drastic population reductions when conditions changed. There are currently more elk than there is food. Last year between 100 and 200 elk starved to death inside the monument. Left alone, the elk population eventually will reach equilibrium, Frenzen says, and meanwhile, "The coyotes are singing a happier tune." So are the ravens, bears, and cougars who also feed on the elk carcasses.

But most people in the group recoil at the sight of the elk. They see the carcasses not as evidence of the wonder of the natural order but as two pitiful dead creatures. Even Frenzen is not immune to such feelings. "It was pretty sad to see elk out here last winter," he says. "They couldn't even get up, they were so weak." Local people were so affected by the sight of the dying elk they hauled bales of hay up the mountain and left them along the roads.

And emotions have been complicated further. Indian tribes throughout the state have exerted what they regard as their treaty rights to hunt the elk. In 1998 tribal hunters shot two elk inside the monument in plain view of tourists at a scenic viewpoint, setting off a bitter legal battle in the courts.

For a short time after Mount St. Helens erupted, a new sense of wariness extended north and south along the rest of the Cascade Range, from Mount Garibaldi to Lassen Peak. The snowcapped mountains on the horizon were no longer viewed as pretty backdrops but as active volcanoes— any one of which could erupt with devastating force at any time. But in a remarkably short time, that wariness faded. Even in the little towns closest to the volcano—Cougar, Randle, Amboy—which 20 years ago looked like scenes from *Apocalypse Now*, the memories are slipping away. In public high schools, the eruption is nearly as remote as the Civil War. None of the students is old enough to have personal memories of the event, nor are some of the teachers.

Even Van Youngquist says he sometimes worries that the sense of danger of the volcano may be lost. "People have short memories," he said. "They

The monument serves as a classroom. Students from the University of Washington *(left)* on the south side of the volcano measure small conifers within a grid of tree plots. They learn about forest rebirth dynamics through hands-on experience. College interns *(right)* track the return of plant life by remeasuring permanent vegetation plots, careful to note all species on this plot west of Castle Lake.

forget the ash falls and mud flows. I don't look at it as a threat day to day, but you have to be aware of the fact that that thing could wake up again."

As a consultant for the tourism industry, Youngquist, increasingly finds himself at meetings with people too young to have any idea of what went on in 1980. "A good many of these kids weren't even born then," he said. "They don't understand what people went through."

After the eruption, the federal government insisted that Cowlitz County forbid building on land threatened by mudflows and future eruptions, but that building moratorium has since been lifted. The Toutle River valley has turned into one of the hottest development areas in southwest Washington. Affluent young families with jobs as far away as Portland and Olympia are colonizing the area, looking for rural solitude within commuting distance.

The corridor bristles with signs advertising real estate for sale and new housing developments. At one building site, a 19-acre development named St. Helens Village, a $359,000 "Belmont" model home is open for inspection. A brochure in a plastic case out front invites prospective buyers to "Lay back and enjoy the master bath jetted tub looking out the window at the beautiful mountain view."

Inside, a young carpenter with brilliant blue eyes and a tall brush cut puts the final touches on trim and cabinets. He scoffs at the idea that people

149

Left: Near Windy Pass, red elderberry fruit create an eye-catching contrast to the still predominately gray landscape around the national monument. The berries also provide food for local birds. *Above:* A small stream's outflow seeps through what was once a dry pumice plain. A verdant selection of mosses, willows, and fireweed collect around this oasis.

who wind up living in the house might be in potential danger. "It would never reach here. They might get a little ash, but that's about it."

Not a single person who has looked at the house has expressed any concern about living next to an active volcano, he says. "If it ever did go off," he laughs, "think of what a great view they'd have."

Nature is an active accomplice in concealing the danger of Mount St. Helens. Mudflows that so recently looked like disasters are now groves of tightly packed alder and cottonwood trees. What were once raw chasms in the ash now look like old, weathered stream beds. The landscape has changed so fast, in fact, that an organization called the Mount St. Helens Creation Information Center has set up shop along the Spirit Lake Memorial Highway, declaring that the rapid change in the volcanic landscape is proof that the Bible was right: the Earth is only thousands of years old.

Everywhere, time has smoothed the volcano's rough edges. Except in the area closest to the crater, it takes an educated eye to discern that there was an eruption here at all. The land inside the monument has become a mosaic of young forests interspersed with meadows. Killdeer and red-winged blackbirds dart over fields lit by a kaleidoscope of blooms: fireweed and pearly everlasting, penstemon and lupine. Alders and cottonwoods by the millions flourish along the mudflows, effectively masking the ravages of such a short time ago. The crater itself and the plain of pumice that spreads out from it are least changed, but even here, a cloak of vegetation softens the starkness.

Nature is going full speed ahead to hide the evidence—and so is the timber industry. Ten years after the eruption, reforestation on private land in the blast zone had progressed so far that it was hard to tell the devastated area from the reforested clearcuts that cover much of the rest of the Cascade Range. Twenty years after, the new trees have progressed enough so that Weyerhaeuser is already scheduling harvests: in 2025, the company plans to begin logging the first of the 18.4 million seedlings it planted on its land in the blast zone.

But all of this change is deceptive. Scientific detective work inspired by the eruption has led geologists to conclude that Mount St. Helens and the other volcanoes in the Cascade Range have erupted far more often and with far more disastrous consequences than anyone had previously suspected. The present cycle of eruptions in the Cascades, geologists now believe, has been continuing at least since the last time the Earth's magnetic poles reversed, some 770,000 years ago, and there is nothing to indicate that the cycle has stopped. Of the seventeen major volcanoes in the range, only six— Garibaldi in British Columbia; Jefferson, the Three Sisters, Crater Lake, and McLoughlin in Oregon; and Medicine Lake in California—do not exhibit some type of thermal activity. Six others—St. Helens, Baker, Rainier, Hood, Shasta, and Lassen—are all considered very likely to erupt.

No mainstream geologist seriously doubts that Mount St. Helens will erupt again. The only question is: "When?"

In 1989, after years of quiet convinced most geologists that the 1980 series of eruptions had ended, steam and ash explosions started up again. In January 1990, the biggest explosion in six years shook the dome, knocking out seismometers and tiltmeters. The explosion sent ash 90 miles away, dusting the cities of Yakima and Toppenish. More explosions occurred in the winter of 1991.

The ground beneath the volcano shudders constantly, and every so often the palpitations increase abruptly—a sign, geologists say, that fresh magma is moving into the volcano's eruption conduit five miles underground, fueling the mountain for the next explosion. Ordinarily, seismometers detect about 60 earthquakes a month under St. Helens, but in 1995 and then again in 1998, swarms of earthquakes rumbled through. A hundred and sixty-five earthquakes shook the mountain in May 1998, and geologists discovered carbon dioxide leaking out of cracks in the crater floor, raising the suspicion that a new eruption could be imminent. In June there were 318 earthquakes, and in July there were 445. Then things returned to normal.

Technological advances in volcano-monitoring equipment since the 1980 eruption have given geologists more confidence in predicting when volcanic

Hiker and landscape on Norway Pass Trail. More lush than other places in the area, this vegetation survived because it was protected by the snow during the blast.

activity is likely to occur. The impromptu encampment of geologists who converged on Vancouver in 1980, working 16-hour days, catnapping in sleeping bags on the floor and feeding on junk food, has evolved into the U.S. Geological Survey's sophisticated Cascades Volcano Observatory. The observatory is part research lab and part fire station; a rapid response team stationed here can respond within 24 hours to threatening volcanic activity anywhere in the world. Scientists at the observatory are constantly refining tools that detect the subtle ground movements that typically precede volcanic eruptions. New computer technology and microelectronics have made it possible to measure movements down to the barest quiver. New tiltmeters, for example, are so sensitive that they can detect changes in slope down to fractions of a single microradian. (To grasp the concept of a microradian, imagine a carpenter's level a half mile long. Slipping a dime under one end of the level would change its tilt by approximately one microradian.) New global positioning system (GPS) receivers use data transmitted by orbiting satellites to provide more precise readings of vertical and horizontal movements than were ever before possible. And new computer-assisted analyses of the amplitude and frequencies of earthquakes provide instant computer images that track the underground movement of magma. Readings from these monitors can be telemetered to a central receiving site and automatically analyzed almost as quickly as they occur. Like doctors on call, geologists at the observatory take turns carrying a beeper programmed to go off when danger thresholds are reached.

The succession of a blowdown on Windy Ridge, *from top to bottom,* 1982, 1994, and 1999. A multitude of grasses and wildflowers have emerged around these downed Norway fir, Douglas fir, and hemlock. *Above right:* Wildflowers, three miles from the crater.

But even with such precise measurements, predicting what might happen next at Mount St. Helens is still far from an exact science. And geologists now realize it does not take an eruption to trigger volcanic disasters. Devastating mudflows called lahars can be set off by small avalanches or even by heavy rain—in which case they occur suddenly, without warning.

Lahars are a bigger hazard than eruptions, according to Pat Pringle, a tenacious geological sleuth who works for the Washington State Department of Natural Resources. Most Cascade volcanoes are well inside national forests or national parks, Pringle notes, and their potential blast zones—about 20 miles in any direction—are sparsely populated. But because most of the Cascade volcanoes are permanently covered with snow and ice, they store enormous quantities of water on their summits. An eruption on any of the peaks could send slurries of mud and house-sized boulders surging down river valleys. Most of the rivers that drain the volcanoes flow west toward major population centers, including Seattle, Tacoma, and Portland.

Pringle is an enthusiastic, engaged man, slender and so tall that his colleagues sometimes pretend not to trust the altimeter on his watch because it's so far off the ground. By hacking through underbrush and scrutinizing the deposits of old eruptions, Pringle has found evidence of old mudflows farther from the volcanoes—and deeper—than anyone thought possible. In some cases, the old flows are covered with forests; in others, they're covered with houses, roads, and strip malls. Working just ahead of developers excavating for a new housing development 30 miles downstream from Mount Rainier, Pringle discovered the remnants of an ancient forest buried in an old volcanic mudflow 20 feet deep.

Rainier poses the biggest mudflow problems in the range, Pringle says. It has not erupted as often or as violently as St. Helens in the last few thousand years, but it has produced much bigger mudflows. Because Rainier is the highest mountain in the range (14,410 feet), it has the most ice and snow on its top. The 26 glaciers radiating from its summit contain the equivalent of a cubic mile of water—fifty times more than the amount on Mount St. Helens before it erupted in 1980, and as much as all other Cascade Range volcanoes combined. If all of the ice and snow on Mount Rainier were to melt at once, hydrologists say, the flow of water off the mountain would be equal to the flow of the Columbia River at flood stage for 10 days.

Approximately 100,000 people live on top of Rainier's previous mudflows, Pringle estimates. Judging from Rainier's past eruptions, mudflows that dwarf those at Mount St. Helens would stream down the Nisqually, White, Carbon, Cowlitz, and Puyallup river valleys, burying towns and suburbs and perhaps reaching as far as Tacoma's Commencement Bay—one of Washington State's most heavily industrialized areas.

As recently as 500 years ago a large mudflow traveled more than 35 miles down the Puyallup River. The Osceola Mudflow, a wall of mud hundreds of feet high that thundered down the White River valley between 5,000 and 6,000 years ago, was one of the largest in the history of the planet. It contained more than 2.5 billion cubic yards of material and filled some sections of the valley with mud 800 feet deep. The mud spread out over 125 square miles of Puget Sound lowland, burying the present sites of Auburn, Buckley, and Enumclaw and filling in an arm of Puget Sound that formerly extended through the Puyallup-Duwamish valley.

Mount St. Helens has potential problems of its own. Geologists are worriedly watching as, winter by winter, ice and snow fill the empty bowl of the crater like a big ice-cream cone. By 1999, 80 million cubic meters of snow and ice had built up inside the crater, a greater volume than the amount of material that swept down the north fork of the Toutle in 1980. Geologists say this snowpack is essentially a lahar waiting to happen. Another worrisome possibility is that one of the high mountain lakes created by the flow of avalanche debris in 1980 could break free of the unstable material that now contains it and flush down the Toutle River.

Despite these dangers, the drive to increase tourism on Mount St. Helens continues. Officials from the five counties that surround the mountain are pushing for yet another new road. If the existing Spirit Lake Highway were to be extended eastward 25 miles, they reason, it would open the volcano to a profitable stream of tourist traffic from the east side of the state.

Predicting when such a disaster might happen is impossible, even with all the tiltmeters, satellites, and seismometers in the world. Perhaps more useful than any of those tools is an old Japanese proverb: "A natural calamity," the ancients said, "will strike at about the time the terror of the last one is forgotten."

Along the Hummocks Loop trail, on the west side of the mountain, a Cascades frog sits in a pond. These frogs are a remarkable sign of the mountain's recovery.

GLOSSARY

active volcano: A volcano that is erupting or a volcano that has erupted within historical time and is considered likely to do so in the future.

andesite: Volcanic rock (or lava) that is usually medium grey in color and contains 54 to 62 percent silica and moderate amounts of iron and magnesium. Andesites (named for the Andes Mountains of South America) occur abundantly throughout the western United States.

ash (volcanic): Fine pyroclastic material in fragments less than 4.0 millimeters in diameter. Volcanic ash does not result from common combustion but from the rapidly expanding gases in magma that shatter the rock froth and explode it into the air.

ash cloud: Eruption cloud containing large quantities of volcanic ash.

ashfall: Volcanic ash that has fallen through the air from an ash cloud.

ash flow: An avalanche of volcanic ash and gases, highly heated, traveling down the flanks of a volcano or along a level surface.

avalanche: A large mass of material, such as snow, ice, soil, or rock, falling or sliding rapidly under the force of gravity. A mixture of these materials is called a debris avalanche.

basalt: Volcanic rock (or lava) that is dark in color, contains 45 to 54 percent silica, and generally is rich in iron and magnesium. Typically flows long distances from its source and is the characteristic lava of most shield volcanoes. The outpouring of highly fluid basalts created the vast inland plateaus of Washington and Oregon during the Miocene epoch.

blast zone: The entire area around Mount St. Helens that was affected by the heat and force of the eruption, approximately 234 square miles. Does not include area affected only by ashfall.

blowdown zone: An irregularly shaped area within the blast zone extending from four to seventeen miles from the crater, in which trees were knocked down by the force of the eruption but were not disintegrated or carried away.

carbon dating: The use of carbon 14, a naturally radioactive carbon isotope with atomic mass 14 and a half-life of 5,700 years, to date ancient carbon-containing objects.

crater: A steep-sided, bowl-shaped depression, formed by either explosion or collapse at a volcanic vent and from which gases, rock fragments, or lava are ejected.

dacite: Lava with a high silica content. Dacites are usually slow moving and viscous when erupted and can form flows of exceptional thickness. Glacier Peak and Mount Garibaldi in the Cascade Range are formed principally of dacite lava.

debris avalanche: A rapid slide or flow of unsorted masses of rock and other material. In the May 18, 1980, eruption of Mount St. Helens, the debris avalanche included fragmented cold and hot volcanic rock, water, snow, glacial ice, trees, and some hot pyroclastic material. Most of the eruption's deposits in the upper valley of the North Fork of the Toutle River and near Spirit Lake are from the debris avalanche.

deformation: Changes in the shape or structure of a volcano, typically caused by magma approaching the surface. Used to predict eruptive activity.

dome: A steep-sided, often circular mass of lava extruded from a volcanic vent, with a spiny, rounded, or flat top. Its surface often is rough and blocky because the cooler, outer crust breaks into fragments as the dome grows. The formation of a lava dome in a crater is an indication that the eruptive force is decreasing.

dormant volcano: Literally, "sleeping." A volcano that is not erupting but is considered likely to erupt in the future.

ejecta: Material such as pumice, ash, and rock thrown out from a volcano.

extinct volcano: A volcano that is not presently erupting and is considered unlikely to do so.

fissure: Long fractures on the slopes of a volcano or along the ground that normally produce liquid lava flows but may also produce pyroclastic material. In a fissure eruption the lava spreads out in sheets, and when the eruption is over the eruptive vent is concealed. Fissures, or zones of fissures, may be several miles long. The Columbia River Plateau, which covers most of Washington and Oregon, is believed to have been created by outpourings of lava from fissures.

fumarole: A vent from which fumes or vapors are emitted, often at high temperatures.

geochemistry: The science of the chemical composition and alterations of the earth's crust.

geophysics: The physics of geological phenomena, including fields such as meteorology and seismology.

geology: The scientific study of the origin, history, and structure of the earth.

harmonic tremor: A continuous release of seismic energy typically associated with the underground movement of magma. Different from the sudden release and rapid decrease of seismic energy associated with the more common type of earthquake caused by slippage along a fault.

hydrology: The scientific study of the properties of water and the effects of water on the earth's surface, in the soil and underlying rocks, and in the atmosphere.

inner blast zone: The area directly to the north of Mount St. Helens and most heavily impacted by the heat and blast of the May 18, 1980, eruption. In places it extends as far as eight miles from the crater.

lahar: An Indonesian term for debris flows and mudflows. A flow of water-saturated debris that originates on the flank of an avalanche and sweeps down its slopes into adjacent river drainages.

lava: General term for molten rock that has been erupted onto the earth's surface through a volcanic vent.

lava dome: See *dome.*

lava flow: An outpouring of lava onto the land surface from a vent or fissure. Also, a solidified sheet of rock formed by outpouring lava.

magma: Molten rock charged with varying amounts of gases as it exists beneath the earth's surface.

magnitude: A numerical expression of the amount of energy released by an earthquake, determined by measuring earthquake waves on standardized recording instruments (seismographs). The numerical scale for magnitudes (the Richter scale) is logarithmic rather than arithmetic; therefore, deflections on a seismograph for a magnitude 5.0 earthquake are 10 times greater than those for a magnitude 4.0 earthquake, 100 times greater than for a magnitude 3.0 earthquake, and so on.

mantle: The intermediate layer of the earth between the crust and the core. The mantle is surrounded by the crust and rests on the core at a depth of about 1,800 miles.

Mount St. Helens National Volcanic Monument: Federally designated area consisting of 109,900 acres in the Cascade Range of Washington state, including and surrounding Mount St. Helens. Formed for the protection, study, and enjoyment of volcanic features, it is managed by the U.S. Forest Service. Legislation establishing the monument was passed by Congress in the summer of 1982 and signed by President Ronald Reagan on August 26 of that year.

mudflow: A flow of water-saturated earth that possesses a high degree of fluidity during movement, much like wet concrete. A less-saturated flowing mass is often called a debris flow. A mudflow originating on the flank of a volcano also is called a lahar.

plates: Large slabs or blocks of the earth's crust, which in the theory of plate tectonics are assumed to move about and jostle one another like gigantic ice floes.

plate tectonics: The theory that the earth's crust is divided into a number of large blocks or "plates" that are slowly moving with respect to one another and that many of the structural features of the earth, such as mountains, are formed at the juncture of the plates.

pumice: Light-colored, frothy volcanic rock, usually with a high silica content, formed by the expansion of gas in erupting lava. Commonly perceived as lumps or fragments of pea-size and larger, pumice can also occur abundantly as ash-sized particles. Waterborne pumice can float for many months before becoming waterlogged and sinking.

pyroclastic: A general term applied to volcanic material that has been explosively ejected from a volcanic vent. From the Greek *pyro,* meaning "fire," and *clastic,* meaning "broken."

pyroclastic flow: Lateral flow of a turbulent mixture of hot gases and unsorted volcanic fragments, crystals, ash, pumice, and glass shards, which can move at speeds of 50 to 100 miles per hour. The term also can refer to a deposit formed of pyroclastic material.

Red Zone: The area surrounding pre-eruption Mount St. Helens believed to be most hazardous and to which entry was generally restricted to scientists and law enforcement and/or rescue personnel. The U.S. Forest Service established the first Red Zone on March 25, 1980, closing off the mountain above timberline. Washington Governor Dixy Lee Ray officially established a significantly larger Red Zone on April 30, 1980, which roughly followed the boundary between federal land and private timberland. In a less restrictive "Blue Zone," certain activities, including logging, were allowed during daylight hours.

Richter scale: A logarithmic scale ranging from one to ten, used to express the magnitude, or total energy, of an earthquake. Named for Charles F. Richter, American seismologist, born in 1900.

Ring of Fire: A zone of active, dormant, and recently extinct volcanoes that encircles the Pacific Ocean (and includes the Cascade Range). According to the plate-tectonics theory, volcanoes on the Ring of Fire are caused by the expansion of the Pacific Ocean floor into bordering continents.

scorch zone: Area of standing dead forest at the margin of the blast zone where trees were killed by heat but blast forces were insufficient to knock them over. Zone was typically narrow (100 yards or less) except in the northwestern corner of the blast zone, where it was as wide as two miles.

sediment: Material suspended in water; also, the deposits of material once they drop out of solution.

sedimentation: The act or process of depositing sediment.

seismogram: The record of an earth tremor made by a seismograph. Used in volcanology to determine the depth of earthquakes, and to identify surface events such as gas emissions, avalanches, and harmonic tremor.

seismograph: An instrument for automatically detecting and recording the intensity, direction, and duration of any movement of the ground, especially of an earthquake. Used in volcanology to predict eruptive activity.

seismology: The geophysical science of earthquakes and of the mechanical properties of the earth.

seismometer: A detecting device that receives seismic impulses but does not record them.

shield volcano: A broad, gently sloping volcanic cone composed chiefly of overlapping flows of basaltic lava; Mauna Loa on the island of Hawaii is an example.

stratovolcano: A volcano that emits both pyroclastic material and viscous lava and that builds up a steep conical mound. Also called a composite volcano. All of the tallest Cascade peaks—Rainier, Shasta, Hood, Adams, St. Helens—are stratovolcanoes.

subduction: The process, according to the plate-tectonics theory, by which the earth's crust descends into the mantle.

tephra: A collective term for pyroclastic materials of all types and sizes that are erupted from a crater or volcanic vent and deposited from the air, including ash, cinders, pumice, etc.

tiltmeter: An instrument used to measure horizontal fluctuations of the earth's surface; used in volcanology to measure the deformation of a volcano by magmatic pressure.

vent: An opening in the ground through which volcanic material is ejected. A vent may be long, narrow, and irregular, or simply an individual vertical pipe.

volcano: A vent in the earth's crust through which lava or gases are ejected. Also the accumulation (cone) of material around the vent. Derived from the Latin name *Vulcanus* or *Volcanus,* which was applied in ancient times to an island off the coast of Sicily because it was believed to be the location of the forge of Vulcan.

volcanology: The science concerned with volcanic phenomena.

Vulcan: Roman god of fire and the forge, after whom volcanoes are named.

Glossary compiled in part from Fred M. Bullard, *Volcanoes of the Earth* (Austin: University of Texas Press, 1984); Steven Harris, *Fire & Ice: The Cascade Volcanoes* (Seattle: The Mountaineers and Pacific Search Press, 1980); Bruce L. Foxworthy and Mary Hill, *Volcanic Eruptions of 1980 at Mount St. Helens: The First 100 Days* (U.S. Geological Survey Professional Paper no. 1249, Washington, D.C.: Government Printing Office, 1982).

SUGGESTED READING

Bullard, Fred M. *Volcanoes of the Earth.* Austin: University of Texas Press, 1984.

Crandell, Dwight R., and Donal R. Mullineaux. *Potential Hazards from Future Eruptions of Mount St. Helens Volcano.* U.S. Geological Survey Professional Paper no. 1383-C. Washington, D.C.: Government Printing Office, 1978.

Dryer, Thomas J. "First Ascent of Mount St. Helens." *Northwest Discovery* 1, no. 3 (August 1980): 164–180.

Franklin, Jerry F., James A. MacMahon, Frederick J. Swanson, and James R. Sedell. "Ecosystem Responses to the Eruption of Mount St. Helens." *National Geographic Research* (Spring 1985): 198–216.

Foxworthy, Bruce L., and Mary Hill. *Volcanic Eruptions of 1980 at Mount St. Helens: The First 100 Days.* U.S. Geological Survey Professional Paper no. 1249. Washington, D.C.: Government Printing Office, 1982.

Harris, Stephen L. *Fire & Ice: The Cascade Volcanoes.* Seattle: The Mountaineers and Pacific Search Press, 1980.

Kozloff, Eugene N. *Plants and Animals of the Pacific Northwest: An Illustrated Guide to the Natural History of Western Oregon, Washington, and British Columbia.* Seattle: University of Washington Press, 1978.

Lipman, Peter W., and Donal R. Mullineaux, eds. *The 1980 Eruptions of Mount St. Helens.* U.S. Geological Survey Professional Paper no. 1250. Washington, D.C.: Government Printing Office, 1981.

Rosenfeld, Charles, and Robert Cooke. *Earthfire: The Eruption of Mount St. Helens.* Cambridge: MIT Press, 1982.

Shane, Scott. *Discovering Mount St. Helens.* Seattle: University of Washington Press, 1985.

Williams, Chuck. *Mount St. Helens: A Changing Landscape.* Portland: Graphic Arts Center, 1980.